IT'S NOT *THAT* LINCOLN

THE CURIOUS STORIES BEHIND SAVANNAH'S HISTORIC STREET NAMES

Also by the Author

On the Swing Shift: Building Liberty Ships in Savannah

The House on Gaston: A Savannah Childhood

Stealing Stones

IT'S NOT *THAT* LINCOLN

THE CURIOUS STORIES BEHIND SAVANNAH'S HISTORIC STREET NAMES

BY

TONY COPE

The Abercorn Press

The Abercorn Press
Savannah, Georgia

Cover illustration drawn and published by Augustus Koch in 1891
Cover design by Georgia Hopkins

For Ellen

More than all of the blades of grass

Table of Contents

PREFACE

Savannah has the largest restored historic district in America and it is based on an original plan designed in 1733 by the founder of the Colony of Georgia, James Edward Oglethorpe. Thousands of tourists annually come to visit the historic homes and walk the streets and squares shaded by giant oaks dripping with Spanish moss. Unlike some in other cities, Savannah's historic district is not a giant movie or theatrical set, although it has been used for those purposes many times. It is, instead a living, breathing, vibrant neighborhood. People live and work there and some even go to college there. The streets are alive with tourists staying in the district's many hotels, and visiting restaurants, bars and clubs. Parishioners attend the many historic churches and business people work in attractive office buildings. Students attend various college classes using historic buildings as classrooms and the large number of gracious restored houses are residences for many families. Most drive or walk these streets every day with no thoughts of for whom they were named.

A few may know some of the more obvious names. Probably every first grader knows for whom Oglethorpe Avenue was named. Most would recognize the name Martin Luther King, Jr, some adults would know about Mr. Gwinnett and Mr. Habersham, and Col. Bull of Bull Street. Some, perhaps, think they know the Lincoln for whom another street is named, but who were Bryan, Drayton, Whitaker or Abercorn? What did Harris, Hull, Houston or Gordon do to warrant having a street named for them? This author grew up on Gaston Street, even wrote a book (*The House on Gaston*) about his experiences there, but it wasn't until many years later that he became interested and discovered who Gaston was.

Which two streets were named for women? Which illustrious notables from Savannah's early history surprisingly had no streets named for them? "IT'S NOT *THAT* LINCOLN" answers all of these questions.

This is a book that should interest both those who are visiting the beautiful City of Savannah and those who are fortunate enough to live here and it might even inspire both to discover more about the street names in their own neighborhoods.

ACKNOWLEDGEMENTS

As with any project like this one, many have provided assistance with information, directions to sources and with the actual production of the final publication. Luciana Spracher, the archivist for the City of Savannah, has been of invaluable assistance in providing information from city ordinances and other resources, not only for this book, but also for the previous three. A great debt is owed to the Live Oak Libraries, whose newspaper files have provided a wealth of information, to the Georgia Historical Society, that wonderful source of all things Georgia and to the online services of the Hargrett Library at the University of Georgia. I am also indebted to friends such as Mrs. Dottie Lynch who provided contacts and sources, and to Dr. Julius Hornstein of Savannah and Mr. Rod Hunt of Osage, Minnesota for their encouragement and enthusiasm for this project.

Many thanks also to my daughter, Georgia Hopkins, who designed the cover, served as computer expert and assisted in the proofreading process, and finally to my wife, Ellen, for her contributions and encouragement throughout.

IT'S NOT THAT LINCOLN

INTRODUCTION

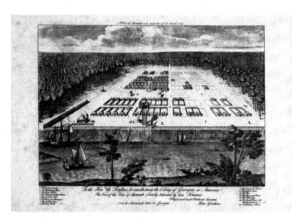

Peter Gordon's Map of Savannah, 1734

In 1966, the downtown area of the City of Savannah was designated a National Historic Landmark District with boundaries running north to south from the Savannah River to Gwinnett Street, and west to east from Martin Luther King, Jr. Boulevard to East Broad Street. It is the largest such district in the United States, covering 2.5 square miles and including more than 1,100 architecturally significant buildings.

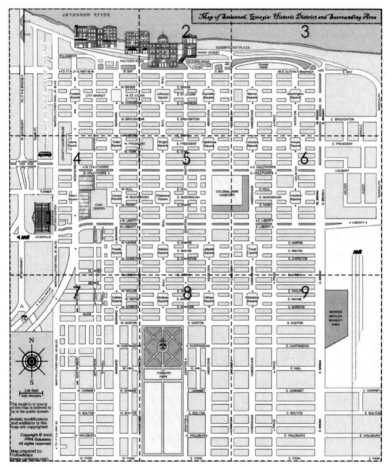

Map of the Historic District

Courtesy of PRN Solutions

EARLY HISTORY OF THE COLONY OF GEORGIA

There were three espoused reasons for the founding of the Colony of Georgia, the thirteenth and last British colony created in America. The first was defensive; to serve as a military buffer between the Colony of South Carolina and the Spanish in Florida. The second was economic, the thought being that the area would be ideal for the growing of indigo, grapes for wine, mulberry trees for the cultivation of silk worms and the production of silk and other products that would relieve Britain's dependence on foreign trade. The third, and perhaps the most well-known to Georgians today, was to take people who had been jailed because of debts, give them an opportunity for a new and productive life in a new land and thereby to reduce the prison populations in Britain.

This third reason was the primary motivating factor for the two men who became the leaders in the establishment of the new colony, Colonel James Edward Oglethorpe and his friend, John Perceval, the 1st Earl of Egmont. Oglethorpe, who began his career as a soldier, was elected a Member of Parliament in 1722 and appointed chairman of that body's committee on prison reform. Horrified by the death from smallpox of a friend who had fallen on hard times and been thrown in prison, and by the squalid, disease-ridden conditions he found, Oglethorpe came up with a plan, supported by his friend John Perceval, which would attempt to address this situation. In 1732, King George II convinced of the efficacy of the plan and perhaps influenced by the fact that the new colony would be named for him, granted the lands between the Altamaha and Savannah Rivers for the colony and named Oglethorpe and Percival as two of twenty-one Trustees for the "Establishing of the Colony of Georgia in America".

With several grants from Parliament and the Bank of England, provisions and tools were purchased and the ship, *Anne*, chartered and stocked with ten tons of "Alderman Parson's best beer" and five tons of wine, one hundred and fourteen settlers left Gravesend, Kent, in November 1732 for the voyage to the new world. These people, however, were not the debtors that Oglethorpe had hoped to save, but were instead "the deserving poor"; carpenters, bakers, tailors, tanners and farmers whose skills would be needed in starting the new colony and who it was hoped could find success in a new environment. Oglethorpe, who by law could not own land or hold office in the colony, nevertheless decided to accompany the settlers on the voyage at his own expense.

During the long voyage many of the settlers, most of whom had never been to sea before, became ill and were treated by Col. Oglethorpe who also provided additional food from his own stocks. Arriving at Charles Town on January 13, 1733, Oglethorpe went ashore to converse with South Carolina Governor Johnson who provided advice and assistance, while the settlers were kept on board for fear that they would decide to stay in the already prosperous colony of South Carolina. A few days later the South Carolina Assembly resolved;

That a present to be given to Mr. Oglethorpe for the new settlers of Georgia forthwith, of an hundred head of breeding cattle and five bulls, as also twenty breeding cows and four boars, with twenty barrels of merchantable rice; the whole to be delivered at the charge of the public, at such a place as Mr. Oglethorpe shall appoint.

Accompanied by Lieutenant Governor and Surveyor General William Bull, the colonists sailed up the Savannah River and on February 12, landed at the high bluff that had been previously selected by Oglethorpe and Bull.

In a letter to the Trustees, Oglethorpe described the site in glowing terms.

The river here forms a half moon, along the south side of which the banks are about 40 feet high and on the top a flat which they call a bluff. The plain high ground extends into the country about five or six miles, and along the river about a mile. Ships that draw 12 feet of water can ride within 10 yards of the bank…the river is pretty wide, the water fresh…you can see its whole course to the sea…and the other way you can see the river for about six miles up into the country.

Others also painted a very rosy picture of the area calling it,

…the most delightful country in the universe, a land watered with noble rivers, stored with useful minerals, abounding with beasts, birds and fish to an incredible degree of plenty.

What the colonists found, however, was a strange land full of alligators, snakes, bugs, bears, sandy soil not favorable for farming and arriving in February, they had yet to experience the heat. Just an hour or so after landing, these tired, cold and disillusioned settlers faced a new and what must have been terrifying ordeal when a contingent of the local Native Americans arrived. One of the colonists, Thomas Causton wrote to his wife saying that the medicine man approached Col. Oglethorpe dancing in, "antick postures" and waving feathered fans around the colonel "whilst the king and others followed, making a very uncouth hollowing."

That these colonists survived that first day as well as the first very difficult months and actually established the colony was due in large part to the leadership of James Oglethorpe and the advice and assistance his new friend, Tomochichi, mico or chief of the small group of Creek Indians already living in the area.

Oglethorpe had met the mico on an earlier surveying visit to the area and two had become immediate friends to the point that Tomochichi accompanied the Colonel on his first trip back to England and was introduced to the Trustees and to King George II. Settlers attempting to establish some of the other colonies in America had not been so fortunate in their relations with Native Americans.

Crane at work on the bluff in the colony

With the colonists safety established and the new town named "Savannah" after the Native American name for the river, Colonel Oglethorpe and William Bull could begin to lay out a plan for the settlement. The actual layout of the town was part of the Trustees' egalitarian view as to how the colony was to be established. Land was to be distributed equally with no large plantations created as had been the case in other colonies. Slavery was prohibited, as was rum and lawyers, and because of the fear of Catholic Spain in Florida, no Catholics were to be allowed to settle in the colony.

The colonel's plan involved the creation of wards. Within each ward there would be four tithing blocks, each with lots for ten houses and four trust lots set aside for public or religious buildings, all surrounding a public square. The squares were designed to provide an open space for residents to congregate, tether livestock and for the training of militias, which each ward was responsible for creating and maintaining. Originally, Oglethorpe laid out plans for six wards. It is to the credit of the planners and politicians who followed, that the plan continued to be used until the middle of the Nineteenth Century.

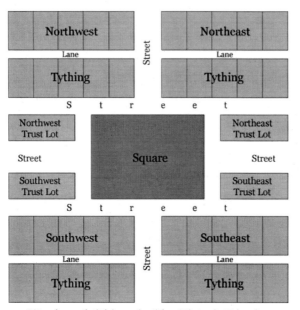

Wards and tithings in The Historic District

THE STREETS OF THE
EARLY COLONIAL PERIOD

In July 1733, Oglethorpe named the first five streets, Bull, Whitaker, Drayton, St. Julian and Bryan for South Carolinians who had provided assistance to the first Georgia colonists.

BULL STREET

Sundial dedicated to William Bull in Johnson Square

"The fashionable promenade of Savannah"

Lt. Governor William Bull was appointed by the South Carolina governor to assist the Georgia colonists because of his surveying skills and his knowledge of the country and the local Native Americans. Prior to the actual arrival of the colonists, he accompanied James Oglethorpe on an exploration of the Georgia coast, rejecting Tybee Island as being too marshy, but finding an ideal site further up the Savannah River. Once the site was selected Bull spent much of that first year helping to survey the town assisting with the construction of houses, organizing the militias and conducting diplomacy with the Native Americans. Along with Joseph Bryan, he furnished twenty of what were euphemistically referred to as "servants" to be employed in such a manner as Oglethorpe deemed most advantageous. While Georgians were prohibited from owning slaves, African Americans from South Carolina provided much of the labor for the establishment of the colony. For many years that contribution to the establishment of the colony was ignored, but today the African American Monument on River Street recognizes Savannah's involvement in the institution of slavery and the contributions made by African Americans to the history, the culture, and the economy of Savannah.

The African American Monument on River Street

William Bull was elected Lt. Governor of South Carolina in 1738 and because of a variety of circumstances served as acting Governor until 1743. His administration was generally considered a successful one even though he had to deal with smallpox and yellow fever epidemics, major fires, droughts and the Stono

Rebellion, the first significant slave insurrection in the colonies.

His son, William Bull Jr., became the first South Carolinian to receive a medical degree and would also serve as Lt. Governor of the colony.

Running north to south, Bull Street has over the years become one of the most beautiful streets in Savannah. J. H. Estill in his *A Guide to Savannah to Strangers* written in 1881, called it "the fashionable promenade of Savannah", saying that

> *"New York has its Broadway and Fifth Avenue, Philadelphia its Chestnut Street, and Washington City its Pennsylvania Avenue each possessing attractions peculiarly its own, and likewise Bull Street has its particular charms. Great shade trees-magnolias, oaks, catalpas – line the curbs of its broad well-paved sidewalks, and their continuation through the lovely squares it crosses, while handsome dwellings and imposing buildings on both sides invite attention."*

The same could be and has been said today. Starting at Bay Street and walking south the visitor would stroll through Johnson, Wright, Chippewa, Madison and Monterey Squares and then the expansive Forsyth Park. It is a trip through an urban forest of majestic trees adorned with necklaces of Spanish moss, passing homes, churches and public buildings of great historical and architectural interest.

The American Planning Association has named Bull Street as one of the ten great streets in America.

WHITAKER STREET

We should, "return to our former Frugality, Temperance and moderate Enjoyment".

This street, running north to south just west of Bull Street was named for Benjamin Whitaker (1698-1751), a lawyer and judge in the Colony of South Carolina who donated one hundred cattle to the first Georgia settlers. Before becoming Chief Justice, Whitaker served on the Committee on Indian Affairs and as Surveyor General. As Surveyor General, he was imprisoned in 1732 for questioning a new law passed by the South Carolina Assembly which allowed speculators to acquire huge areas of land simply by carving notches on trees and without recording the claims in any office.

Whitaker Street looking south

Benjamin Whitaker, concerned about political corruption, was an advocate of "The Great Awakening", a revivalist movement sweeping the colonies in the first half of the 18th Century. This movement was attempt to restore felt religion and simple living among the colonists. To, in his own words, "Return to our former Frugality, Temperance and moderate Enjoyments". He once used his annual address to the Grand Jury to urge his fellow colonists to, "abstain from that luxury and excess which within a few years past, has poured in upon us like a torrent", and so, "greatly contribute to enervate and soften our minds, and to sink us into indolence and inactivity". Advice for today?

Whitaker served as Chief Justice from 1739 until 1749 when he became paralyzed and was removed from office. He died four years later at the age of fifty-three.

DRAYTON STREET

The Drayton Coat of Arms

"A powerful Eighteenth Century matriarch"

Another north to south street just east of Bull Street, Drayton Street was one of the two streets in the Historic District named for a woman. It honors South Carolinian Ann Drayton, who provided for one month, four sawyers whose labor was valued at £60 in South Carolina currency, to assist in the building of houses for the Georgia colonists.

Ann Drayton and her husband arrived in South Carolina in 1676 and established Magnolia Plantation, becoming very wealthy from the cultivation of rice. Her husband died in 1719 and as a widow she became one of the most successful female landowners of the area and of the era. By the time that Ogle-thorpe and the Georgia colonists arrived, she was managing over three thousand acres, ninety-one slaves, 1380 head of cattle and 112 horses, all while raising four children. She would end up owning more than 10,000 acres. Ann Drayton bought bibles, spelling books and horn books from the Georgia Colony in order to educate her slaves. She ran the plantations, bought, sold and leased slaves, and kept the account books: a very unusual situation for a woman at the time. Her wealth and social status allowed her children to enter the highest echelons of society. It also enabled her youngest son, Thomas, Jr. to build Drayton Hall, the restored house and the gardens of which are open to the public today. Britttany L. Lavell in her thesis on the family refers to Ann Drayton as a "powerful Eighteenth Century Matriarch".

BRYAN STREET

The Savannah Bank and Trust Building, 2 East Bryan Street, built in 1911. Once the tallest building in Savannah. Now known as the Johnson Square Business Center

"A man of much force and character and of honored position".
The first west to east street laid out was named for Joseph Bryan Jr., another of the South Carolinians who assisted James Ogle-thorpe and the first Georgia colonists. Bryan spent two months in the new colony with four sawyers and twenty "servants"

(slaves) clearing land and constructing houses.

Bryan, was born in South Carolina about 1697, and later owned a plantation called Providence in Prince William Parish between Pocatalico and Prince William Church. When the Yamassee Tribe which was allied with the Spanish in Florida attacked in that area in 1715, the Bryan family escaped being massacred, as were many settlers, because of the close relationship these Native Americans had had with Joseph Bryan Sr. years earlier.

While few details are known about his life, one historian wrote, "From the education of his children he is judged to have been a man of much force and character and of honored position".

ST. JULIAN STREET

The Pulaski House at St. Julian and Bull Streets in 1920

Asked to greet James Oglethorpe and assure him of South Carolina's "hearty support".

James St. Julian was a prominent South Carolina landowner who operated a large stock farm until his death in 1746. The St. Julian family were Huguenots, the French protestant group who had

had to flee France in the late 17th Century when Louie XIV revoked the Edict of Nantes which had guaranteed their right to worship. After fleeing to Britain, many then immigrated to South Carolina establishing a community near Charles Town.

When the first Georgia colonists arrived at Charles Town, St. Julian was asked by Governor Robert Johnson and his council to greet Colonel Oglethorpe and to assure him of the "hearty support" of South Carolina for the settlement of the new Colony of Georgia.

Soon after Oglethorpe had selected a site and landed the settlers, St Julian spent a month in the new colony directing the construction of houses. Later when Oglethorpe returned to Charles Town in the fall of 1733, to consult with officials there, he left James St. Julian and Francis Scott in charge of caring for the colonists and carrying on the construction work.

Also in 1733, St Julian was appointed by England's Royal Council to survey a six mile square township on the Wateree River which was originally named Fredericksburg in honor of the Prince of Wales.

Over the years, many Huguenot families moved to Savannah and played an important role in the city's history.

DURING THE FIRST TWO YEARS OF THE COLONY'S EXISTENCE, COLONEL OGLETHORPE CONSTRUCTED AND NAMED SEVERAL OTHER STREETS.

BARNARD STREET

Sir John B. Barnard

"The great commoner"

This north to south street was laid out in late 1733 and named by Oglethorpe for Sir John B. Barnard (1685-1764), a merchant, statesman and Member of Parliament for forty years. Along with Oglethorpe he was very active in the attempts to improve the conditions of debtors, hence his interest in the establishment of the Colony of Georgia and his financial contribution to the Trustees' fund for the new colony. He served as the sheriff of London was elected mayor of that city in 1736 and then became a Member of Parliament. As a Whig, he frequently spoke out against the policies of the Prime Minister, Sir Robert Walpole, but was praised for being an honest man of principle throughout his long parliamentary career. William Pitt called him, "The Great Commoner".

Although he was born into a prosperous Quaker family, he was baptized as a child into the Church of England and became a staunch supporter of the Church throughout his life.

A bust of Barnard was installed in the Temple of British Worthies, in the gardens of Lord Cobham's summer house at Stowe. The gardens included among others busts of Sir Francis Drake, William Shakespeare and Elizabeth I.

BROUGHTON STREET

Thomas Broughton

His house on Mulberry Plantation was built over a cellar fort with firing slits.

South of Congress Street and also running west to east, Broughton Street was named in 1733 for Thomas Broughton, a South Carolinian who with four slaves provided carpentry work in the Colony of Georgia for two months.

Broughton was born in Durham England about 1668 and in 1683 married Anne Johnson, whose father would become Governor of the South Carolina colony in 1703. Thomas and Anne arrived in Charles Town in 1695 and created Mulberry Plantation in 1714. Because of the fear of Native American uprisings, the house on the plantation was built over a cellar fort with firing slits in the foundation.

Thomas was named Lt. Governor of the colony in 1731 and in 1735 named himself as acting governor when his father-in-law died. Later his friendship with the Georgia Colony and its residents turned sour and he became very belligerent during a conflict arising over trade with local Native Americans. Brough-ton sided with his South Carolina colleagues in an attempt to drive the Georgians out of the business. When he died in 1737, General Oglethorpe's friend, William Bull, became governor and the problem was resolved.

CONGRESS STREET
STATE STREET
PRESIDENT STREET

Frederic Louis, Prince of Wales
Portrait by Philip Mercier

King George II
Portrait by Thomas Hudson

William Augustus, Duke of Cumberland
Portrait by Joshua Reynolds

"obnoxious names"

Congress Street was laid out in 1733 just south of St. Julian Street and running west to east. It was originally named Duke Street by

Oglethorpe for Duke William Augustus, Duke of Cumberland and the third son of King George II. State Street, just south of Congress and created in the same year, was originally named Prince Street for Frederic Louis, Prince of Wales. Also laid out in 1733, President Street was at first called King Street.

These were not names that would be tolerated after the hard-fought victory over the Crown in the American Revolution. All were changed to reflect a distaste for anything British. An ordinance passed by the city council in 1803 stated that:

Whereas, the names and titles of King, Prince and Duke are unknown to the institutions of Georgia or the United States and the permitting or suffering streets in this city to still be called by those obnoxious names reflects highly on the police thereof, be it therefore ordained by the mayor and aldermen of the City of Savannah…that the streets now called by the following…King Street, Prince Street and Duke Street shall hereafter be called by the names following…King Street shall be called President Street, Prince Street shall be called State Street and Duke Street shall be called Congress Street.

It was probably providential that George II for whom the State was named was a strong early supporter of the new colony or the name of the State might have been changed to perhaps Washington, Jefferson or even Franklin.

YORK STREET

Ernest Augustus, Duke of York
Artist unknown

"Believed to be Homosexual, Ernest Augustus never married."

Named for the Duke of York by Oglethorpe in 1733, for some reason this street was not renamed as were the others with royal connotations. There is some speculation that this was because the Royal colony of New York retained its name after becoming a State following the Revolutionary War.

Ernest Augustus was born in Hanover in 1674 and was the younger brother of George I of England. A soldier under Emperor Leopold I, he fought in the Nine Years War against the French and at the Siege of Lille in 1708 during the War of Spanish Succession.

He was a prominent member of his brother's court in Hanover and when George acceded to the British throne in 1714, Ernest became regent in all but name in Hanover. It is speculated that his influence was instrumental in George Frederick Handel being given the post of Kapellmeister at that court.

Ernest followed his brother to London and stayed for several years as the King's close advisor. In 1716, he was created Duke of York and Albany and Earl of Ulster. Two years later he was made a Knight of the Garter. Ernest Augustus died on August 14, 1728, in Osnabruck and was buried there. He never married or had any children and it was believed that he was homosexual.

OGLETHORPE AVENUE

General James Edward Oglethorpe
Photo by the author

Giving a chance to England's "Worthy Poor"

James Oglethorpe did not name this street after himself. By all indications he wasn't that kind of person and in fact, during his ten years in Georgia, nothing in the colony was named for him.

Oglethorpe did lay out this west to east street in 1733, and named it, South Boundary to reflect the fact that it marked the city limits at the time and would do so until the post-colonial expansion of the town. It would be renamed as South Broad Street, then changed again in 1820, to Market Street as there was, for a number of years, a market operating along the island in the center of the street. The final name change took place on April 7, 1897, when the city council decided to honor the founder of the colony. James Edward Oglethorpe was a soldier, politician, humanitarian and philanthropist. He was born in London on December 22, 1696, the son of Theophilis and Eleanor Oglethorpe, both ardent Jacobites. James served for thirty two years as a Member of Parliament where he advocated the equality of all British subjects in the Empire, opposed slavery, and pushed for prison reform, an interest which led directly to the founding of the Colony of Georgia.

His family's pro Jacobite sympathies which he did not share, would get him into serious trouble in 1745 during the Jacobite Uprising. His troops fought with the Duke of Cumberland's army at the battle at Preston and he was court martialed for failing to aggressively pursue Bonnie Prince Charlie's forces as they escaped back to Scotland. During the trial some suggested that this failure was due to Jacobite leanings, but he was acquitted and while he was never given a command again, he continued to be promoted and died as the highest ranking general in the British Army.

In his later years, Oglethorpe became friends with Dr. Samuel Johnson and was a member of the Literary Club which included among others, Johnson, his biographer James Boswell, the painter Joshua Reynolds, Edmund Burke, playwright Oliver Goldsmith, the historian, Edward Gibbons and the economist, Adam Smith among others.

General Oglethorpe died at the age of eighty-nine on June 30, 1785.

ABERCORN STREET

The Henry VII Chapel at Westminster Abbey where James Hamilton, Sixth
Earl of Abercorn is entombed

An ancestor of Diana, Princess of Wales

Abercorn was the last street created and named by Oglethorpe.
Running north to south just east of Drayton Street, it was named
for James Hamilton, Sixth Earl of Abercorn (1661–1734) who
initially provided £100, a large sum at the time, to help under-
write the cost of transporting the colonists to Georgia and until
his death was a prominent benefactor of the Georgia Colony. A
Scot, who was appointed to the Privy Council of Ireland by King
James II, Hamilton switched allegiances to William of Orange
and served in the defense of Londonderry in 1689 during the
Williamite War. Elected as a Member of the Irish Parliament for
Tyrone, on the death of his second cousin he became The Sixth
Earl of Abercorn, Baron Hamilton of Strabane. He continued to
live in Ireland and amassed an estate of 76,000 acres in the
Counties Tyrone and Donegal.

Abercorn Street today is the longest street in Savannah, extending far beyond the boundary of the Historic District, continuing from Bay Street near the river all the way to the southern part of the county.

BAY STREET

"Broad and beautiful Bay Street"

It is difficult to determine exactly when and if Bay Street was actually laid out. It may be that because of Oglethorpe's design for the town, it wasn't planned, it was just there. As the first street over the river above the bluff, it was originally called The Strand. Francis Moore, who sailed for Georgia in late 1735 in the same ship on which James Oglethorpe made his return to Savannah, arrived in the colony in February 1736. He wrote in his description of the colony that,

> ...care was taken to allow for there being a very wide Strand between the first row of Houses and the River. From this Strand there is a very pleasant Prospect, you see the River wash the Foot of the Hill, which is a hard, clear, sandy Beach...

At some later date, the name was changed to Bay Street and during the 19th century it became the primary route for plantation owners bringing cotton, rice, tobacco and naval stores to the wharves on the river to be shipped to the North and to Europe. J.H. Estill in his "Guide to Savannah" published in 1881, described the street as

> ...broad and beautiful Bay Street...with its long vista of commercial housed and offices, its double row of shade trees, its crowd of vehicles of every description and bustling sidewalks all indicative of commercial enterprise, energy and activity.

Several years later, G.A. Gregory wrote,

Bay Street is the great commercial thoroughfare, and is lined with mercantile houses, banks and business offices. The Custom House, The City Exchange, the post office and the Cotton Exchange are all on "The Bay".

Today, Bay Street has been extended from East Broad all the way to the West Side of Chatham County. In the Historic District, while the Custom House and the Cotton Exchange, now a Masonic hall, are still there, the old offices have been replaced, often in the same buildings, by hotels, businesses, restaurants, upmarket shops, the City Hall, and parks. Two of the most interesting features of the street are the Washington Guns presented to the City by George Washington after a visit in 1791 and the twenty-five foot tall Old Harbor Light, a former aid to navigation on the river, erected in Emmet Park in 1858.

The Washington Guns
Photo by Brent Boyd
Courtesy of The City of Savannah

The Old Harbor Light in Emmet Park

Courtesy Kudzuvine

After Oglethorpe's construction and naming of Abercorn Street in the town, no new streets were laid out until after the Revolutionary War. In 1791, the newly organized city council began a rapid extension of the city's boundaries with the creation of several new wards and eight new streets.

LINCOLN STREET

General Benjamin Lincoln
By Charles Wilson Peale

"Sir, General Lincoln was never asleep when it was necessary for him to be awake."

This is the street that generated the idea for the title of this book. Many visiting Savannah, and probably many locals, think that this street was named for President Abraham Lincoln. There are streets, towns, and parks all over the country named for America's 16th President, but rarely in the South and certainly not in Savannah. First of all, President Lincoln wasn't born until 1809, eighteen years after this street was named. Secondly, the City of Savannah, located in the Deep South, which sent many sons to fight and die in the War Between the States and saw much of the State of Georgia (although not the city itself) ravaged during Sherman's "March to the Sea", would never have named a street for that President.

When Lincoln was assassinated, the city fathers dutifully draped the squares in black, conducted prayer services and were outwardly very mournful. Savannah at the time, however, was a city under Union Army control and this show of sorrow was probably just that, a show. Most Savannahians who blamed Lincoln for the war and all of the suffering that they had endured, quietly rejoiced at his death as illustrated by the statement of one woman that the president's death was "one sweet drop among so much that is painful".

Lincoln Street which runs from the river to Victory Drive, was actually named for General Benjamin Lincoln (1733-1810), a Revolutionary War hero born in Hingham, Massachusetts. This Lincoln commanded the Southern Department of the Continental Army leading the combined French and American armies at the unsuccessful Siege of Savannah and fighting at Charleston, Saratoga and Yorktown. The General was treated very badly when surrendering to Lord Cornwallis at Charleston. Later, when surrendering at Yorktown, Cornwallis was so mortified at his defeat that he sent his second in command to present his sword to General Washington. Washington refused and indicated that it should be presented to General Lincoln.

General Lincoln suffered from narcolepsy and would often fall asleep writing dispatches or during staff meetings. When a gentleman disparaged the General "for always falling asleep", his aide, Major William Jackson, replied, "Sir, Gen. Lincoln was never asleep when it was necessary for him to be awake".

Lincoln County in Georgia is also named for General Benjamin Lincoln.

HABERSHAM STREET

James Habersham

He was, "one of the sweetest, purist, most useful and noblest of a long line of colonial worthies".

From missionary to one of the wealthiest men in the colony, James Habersham exemplified one of the three main goals the Trustees espoused for establishing the Colony of Georgia. The street which bears his name was part of the expansion in 1791 and runs north to south just east of Lincoln Street.

Habersham who became a member of the colonial council and a Royal governor of Georgia from 1771 to 1773, was born in Beverley, Yorkshire, England in 1712 and came to the Georgia Colony in 1738 at the request of George Whitefield to be a missionary and schoolmaster. With Whitefield he helped to establish the Bethesda Orphanage and for several years served as that institution's superintendent and financial officer.

Having spent several years as a merchant in London, Habersham's interests in the colony soon turned to the more secular career of tradesman. In 1744, with Francis Harris he established an "unpretentious place of business" under the bluff at the edge of the Savannah River. At first the two men bought lumber, poultry, hogs, skins, whatever was produced by local farmers and traded with Charles Town, but in 1749 they established the first truly successful commercial venture in the colony. Habersham and Harris loaded a vessel with lumber, skins, hogs and produce and shipped the £10,000 cargo to a firm in London. Shortly thereafter, the firm established commercial relations with Philadelphia, New York and Boston. Charles C. Jones, Jr. wrote in his *History of Savannah* that

> *So successful were the operations of this enterprising firm that the colony materially increased in wealth and in the enjoyment of comforts to which the inhabitants had hitherto been strangers".*

Those operations also materially increased the wealth of Habersham himself as he used his profits to establish a plantation (by this time allowed in the colony) and planted 15,000 acres in rice. As a plantation owner, Habersham was instrumental in having the original ban on slavery in the colony overturned, owned two hundred slaves himself and became one of the largest traders in slaves in the colony. At the time of his death in 1775, he was considered the third wealthiest man in the colony.

Habersham did not support the calls for Independence which put him at odds with his three sons, but he had always told them that he would not impress his own political or religious views upon them and as he died just at the beginning of the War of Independence there were no family issues. Although he was not in favor of Independence, his service to the colony through the positions he held and through the creation of wealth when it was struggling to survive was instrumental in enabling Georgia to separate from the crown and eventually become a prosperous State.

Charles C. Jones Jr wrote of Habersham that was, "one of the sweetest, purist, most useful and noblest of a long line of colonial worthies". This, notwithstanding his involvement with slavery.

PRICE STREET

The Siege of Savannah

"...a man of eminent abilities"

Price Street was named for Revolutionary War hero, Lt. Charles Price who was killed on the governor's plantation just opposite his own home during the Siege of Savannah in 1779. Before the war he was one of the first lawyers in the colony, a profession which had been banned during the period when Georgia was a Trust Colony. He served as prothonotary (chief court clerk), as a member of the General Assembly and as Crown Attorney. James Jackson, himself a Revolutionary War hero and Governor of Georgia recorded in his papers remarks by General Lachlan McIntosh who stated;

> *Mr. John Jones of Sunbury was killed as also Mr. Charles Price, both of them highly lamented and the latter a man of eminent abilities. This loss has been severely felt in Georgia; he was one of the best lawyers perhaps in the United States and possessed as good a heart as he did a clear head and sound judgement*

HOUSTON STREET

John Houston

An opportunity missed...for the right reason.

This is a story of what could have been; a decision made that excluded the name John Houston from the ranks of American immortals. Houston could have been the 57th signer of the Declaration of Independence.

Located just east of Price Street, Houston Street was named for John H. Houston. Spelled and pronounced over the years as Hew-ston, Who-ston, Howston and You-ston, he pronounced it House-ston and that's the accepted pronunciation today. One of the shorter streets in the Historic District, it runs only from Bay Street to Liberty Street.

John Houston (1744-1796) was born in St. George's Parish near the modern town of Waynesboro. He was educated and read Law in Savannah and was a practitioner in the city of that profession for many years. He became an early advocate of Independence and was one of the founders of the Committee of Correspondence in Savannah, formed to support the Boston colonists in their resistance to the intolerable activities of the British Parliament. Houston was appointed to the Second Continental Congress, but did not attend, electing to stay at home to thwart the activities of the Rev. John Zubly. Zubly, the minister of the Independent Presbyterian Church and a staunch supporter of the Crown had left the Congress to return home and inform the Royal Governor of the delegation's "treason". By not attending, Houston thus missed the opportunity to become the fourth Georgia signer of the Declaration of Independence.

In 1778, Houston became the second revolutionary governor and the first to have been born in Georgia. That same year, he took control of the Georgia militia and led an abortive attack on the British in St. Augustine. The attack failed because of Houston's disagreements with General Robert Howe, Commander of the Continental Army in the South. When the British captured Savannah, Houston was forced to flee, returning after the war to serve a term as governor of the new State in 1784. In 1790, he became the first elected Mayor of Savannah and would later serve as a Justice of the Superior Court of Georgia. In his private life, Houston was married to the daughter of Jonathan Bryan, brother of Joseph Bryan for whom Bryan Street is named. The couple built a house at White Bluff where he died in 1796.

EAST BROAD STREET

Location of the Oldest House in Georgia.

In 1791, the Savannah City Council passed an ordinance stating, "The street running north and south on the outer part of the East common and separating that from the Trustees' Garden shall be called East Broad." One of the few streets not named for a person, East Broad still has a very interesting history. The Trustees Garden mentioned in the ordinance was created just four months after the first colonists arrived in 1733. Ten acres, located on a hillside near the river and on the northern end of what would later become East Broad Street, were set aside to grow crops that would free England from its dependency on countries like Italy for olives, citrus and wine grapes, China for silk and Spain for coffee, cocoa and quinine. Attempts were also made to grow ipecacuhana, an emetic and to cultivate the cochineal insect used to produce scarlet dye for court dress and uniforms.

The Trustees' Garden being developed

It was thought by the Trustees that the geography and warm climate of the new colony would be ideal for this purpose and the Garden became the first agricultural experiment station in the Western Hemisphere. Within ten years, however, it was deemed a failure, and for some of the very same reasons that had created the expectations of success. The climate was too hot, there were never enough people trained in the necessary farming skills and support from London waned. By 1740, the land had been converted to residential use. The "Herb House" built in 1734 for the project's gardener is the oldest house still in existence in the State of Georgia. Today it forms one of the structures of the Pirate's House Restaurant, famous both for its food and for its connection with the book, *Treasure Island* by Robert Louis Stevenson.

In 1762, Fort Wayne was built on the site of the Trustees Garden overlooking the river. Originally named Fort Savannah, it was constructed as part of the defenses against the Spanish in Florida, but it wasn't until the Revolutionary War that it became of some importance. Captured by the British at the beginning of the war and then recaptured by American Forces several years later it was renamed for the Revolutionary War hero General "Mad Anthony" Wayne. To long-time Savannah residents it has always been known as the "Old Fort".

In the 1830's many Irishmen were brought to Georgia to build the railroads and as many moved into the Old Fort area, the term "Old Fort" began to be used in a less than complimentary way. The area also had a large African-American population, the two groups sharing the links of poverty and prejudice.

East Broad like West Broad became a busy commercial and entertainment area for African-Americans as most were not allowed to live in the Historic District. The Melody Theater, the first fully air-conditioned theater for African-Americans in the city, with its large auditorium and complete soda shop opened in March of 1946, on the corner of Hall Street and East Broad. The East Side Theater also showing African-American oriented films, opened in late 1946, a block further south on Gwinnett Street and East Broad. With integration both theaters eventually closed and the character of the street changed dramatically.

Today, the northern area of East Broad is known as Trustees Garden Village and along with upmarket residences, features many trendy restaurants and shops. Further south is the Clarence Thomas Center for Historic Preservation and the historic St. Benedict the Moor Catholic Church, originally constructed in 1874 and replaced with a new building in 1949.

MARTIN LUTHER KING JR. BOULEVARD

Dr. Martin Luther King, Jr.

"I Have a Dream"

In 1791, when East Broad marked the eastern boundary of the town, an ordinance of the city council delineated the western boundary: "and the street running in the same direction of north and south, on the outer part of the west common, and separating that from Yamacraw and St. Gaul's lots shall be called West Broad Street."

In the early 1800's West Broad was a fashionable address, but by the middle of the century it had developed a reputation for crime and blight as poor Irish immigrants moved in alongside the already established African-American community. By the middle of the Twentieth century the Irish had moved on or assimilated into the white community in the Historic and Victorian districts and the street became the center for African-American culture and entrepreneurship in the city. African American owned businesses, pharmacies, the Star and Dunbar movie theaters, and a number of local banks created what came to be called, "The Wall Street of Black America". A Morehouse College survey in the 1940's indicated that there were 177 African-American businesses and 27 African-American owned restaurants in Savannah, most congregated on West Broad. Fifteen of the twenty-two African-American doctors and dentists in the city also had their practices on this street.

Towards the end of the 20th Century, the street began to change again. The iconic Union Station and 650 feet of storefronts were torn down to accommodate the Interstate16 flyover. New hotels, fast food restaurants and college dormitories, classrooms and galleries replaced the mom-and-pop businesses, restaurants and clubs that for many years had made the street a mecca for African-American culture. Today the street features many of the city's most visited attractions including The Savannah Visitors Center, the Savannah History Museum, The Battlefield Park, the Georgia State Railroad Museum, the Ships of the Sea Maritime Museum housed in the historic Scarbrough House and the Ralph Mark Gilbert Civil Rights Museum featuring exhibits of the street's earlier African American history.

In 1990, the street was renamed in honor of Dr. Martin Luther King, Jr. Born in Atlanta in 1929, King became a Baptist minister and a key figure in the American Civil Rights Movement. A founder of the Southern Christian Leadership Conference in 1957, he led the 1963 March on Washington where he delivered his "I have A Dream" speech before the thousands gathered in front of the Lincoln Memorial. He organized marches throughout the South and in 1964 was awarded the Nobel Peace Prize.

Dr. King was assassinated in 1968 in Memphis and after his death was awarded the Presidential Medal of freedom, and the Congressional Gold Medal. Hundreds of streets around the country have been named in his honor and the Martin Luther King, Jr. Memorial on the National Mall in Washington D.C. was dedicated to him in 2011. In 1986, Dr. Martin Luther King, Jr. Day was established as a federal holiday and the parade on that day is one of the major annual events in Savannah.

MONTGOMERY STREET

Rich.ᵈ Montgomery

"Never so happy in all my life…this cannot last, it cannot last".
This is one of the streets named for someone who never set foot in Savannah. Laid out in 1791, just east of and running parallel to Martin Luther King, Jr. Boulevard, Montgomery Street was named for General Richard Montgomery, killed in 1775 in the American attack on Quebec during the Revolutionary War. Born in 1738 in Swords, County Dublin, Ireland, he studied at Trinity College and joined the British Army to fight in the French and Indian War in the Colonies. At the end of that war he resigned his commission and returned to America with the intention of becoming a farmer. In 1773 he married Janet Livingston from a wealthy family and declared, "Never so happy in all my life…this cannot last, it cannot last…"

Tied by marriage to the Livingston family who were supporters of independence, Montgomery began to see himself more American than British and to consider the British government to be oppressive. When the war began, he joined the patriots and was commissioned a brigadier general. He led the invasion of Canada, captured Fort St John and was promoted to major general. During the ill-fated battle of Quebec while charging a blockhouse with his sword drawn and reportedly shouting, "Men of New York, you will not fear to follow where your general leads you", Montgomery was killed by cannon grapeshot.

The Death of General Montgomery
By John Trumbull

The British buried him with full military honors and American prisoners in attendance stated that he was "a beloved general" with "heroic bravery" and "suavity of manners" who held the confidence of the entire army.

Montgomery's superior, Gen. Schuyler wrote in a letter to Congress and to General George Washington, "In the death of this gentleman, America has sustained a heavy loss, as he approved himself as a steady friend of her rights and of ability as to render her the most essential services". His death was kept a secret for fear of the loss of morale among the military and civilian population.

In 1818, the Governor of New York had the general's remains brought to New York City where they were interred next to his monument in St. Paul's Chapel.

Along with the street in Savannah, fourteen States have counties named for General Montgomery. Many schools and streets throughout the country as well as the city of Montgomery, Alabama bear his name. A number of U.S. navy ships have also carried his name. A Liberty ship built in Florida, the S.S. Richard Montgomery, broke apart and sank in the Thames Estuary in the United Kingdom during World War II and is still a hazard to navigation there.

JEFFERSON STREET

Thomas Jefferson
By Rembrandt Peale

"I cannot live without books."

Perhaps, one of the three most recognizable names (along with Washington and Franklin) arising out of America's struggle for independence was that of Thomas Jefferson. The last of the streets laid out in 1791 was named for this very accomplished individual, the author of the Declaration of Independence who ten years later, became the third President of the United States. Just east of Montgomery Street, Jefferson Street, too, runs north to south.

For over five decades, Thomas Jefferson served America as a philosopher, architect, horticulturist, educator, inventor and public official. Born in 1743 in Shadwell in the Colony of Virginia, he inherited 5000 acres when his father died in 1757. He began building his home in 1768 on a hilltop called Monticello

(Italian for Little Mountain) overlooking his plantation. Graduating from the College of William and Mary, Jefferson studied Law and obtained his license to practice. In 1772, he married Martha Wayles Skelton and the couple had ten children before she died in 1782. One has to wonder if having ten children in ten years contributed to her death.

Jefferson's political career began when he served as a delegate to the Virginia House of Burgesses from 1769 to 1775. At the beginning of the Revolutionary War, he was elected as a delegate to the Second Continental Congress and was asked to write a draft for The Declaration of Independence. After some revisions by members of the Congress, the Declaration was ratified on July 4, 1776. His preamble and the words "all men are created equal" are among the most quoted in the English language.

During the war, Jefferson served again in the Virginia House of Burgesses and was elected to two terms as governor of the new State. After the war, he was appointed to the new Congress of the Confederation, and was then chosen to join Benjamin Franklin and John Adams as a minister to France. In 1789, he was asked by President Washington to become the nation's first Secretary of State and during his tenure he was involved in determining that the nation's capital would be located on the Potomac River.

Jefferson ran, but lost the election in 1796 for the presidency by three electoral votes to John Adams thus becoming vice president. He would run against Adams again in 1800, this time being elected by the House of Representatives after a tie in the Electoral College.

Highlights of his first term included victory in the First Barbary War, the Louisiana Purchase which doubled the size of the United States, the initiating of the Lewis and Clark and several other expeditions to explore the western frontier and the securing of alliances with many Native American tribes. Elected to a second term in 1804, Jefferson's popularity waned because of his conflict with Aaron Burr and the ineffectiveness of his embargoes against the British over their impressment of American sailors. He decided not to seek a third term and when leaving office stated that he felt like "a prisoner, released from his chains".

After retiring from public life, Jefferson continued to improve his home, Monticello, and in 1819 founded the University of Virginia. A voracious reader and lover of books, by 1814 he had amassed a library of 6,500 volumes, but deeply in debt he sold 6,000 books to the government for $23,950 to reestablish the Library of Congress which had been burned by the British. He did use some of the money to pay off a few debts, but began collecting again for his own library. He confessed to John Adams, "I cannot live without books".

Thomas Jefferson's ideas on slavery are confusing to say the least. As a young lawyer, he took on a number of cases for slaves seeking freedom, stating that "everyone comes into the world with a right to his own person and using it at his own will". This thought was stated more succinctly as, "all men are created equal", in the Declaration of Independence. As governor of Virginia in 1779, he proposed the gradual voluntary training and resettlement of slaves to the Virginia legislature and in 1807 he signed an Act of Congress prohibiting the importation of slaves. In his book, *Notes on the State of Virginia*, he called slavery a "moral evil". Jefferson, however, owned several plantations and a number of slaves himself and recent DNA tests have shown that it is probable that he had several children by his slave, Sally Hemings.

Thomas Jefferson died at Monticello on July 4, 1826, the fiftieth anniversary of the signing of the Declaration of Independence. Like George Washington and Abraham Lincoln, Jefferson is remembered throughout the United States through the naming of streets, towns and cities, schools and universities. He is one of the four presidents whose faces are carved on Mount Rushmore and the Jefferson Memorial in Washington, D. C. was built in his honor and dedicated in 1943. In Georgia, Jefferson County is also named for the former president.

In 1801, Savannah began expanding to the south, with four new streets laid out.

HULL STREET

Commodore Isaac Hull
Portrait by Rembrandt Peale

"...a bundle of pine boards sailing under a bit of striped bunting"

The Savannah City Council laid out this west to east street just south of Oglethorpe Avenue and originally named it Chatham Street for William Pitt, the Earl of Chatham, who was a champion of equal rights for British colonists in America. It was renamed in 1815 for Commodore Isaac Hull the naval hero of the War of 1812. The Earl of Chatham was not ignored for long however, as in 1847, a square was named him.

Isaac Hull was born in Connecticut in 1773 to a father who was a merchant marine captain. He went to sea as a cabin boy and showed early signs of bravery and heroism by saving the life of his captain by supporting him in the water after their ship sank. Hull rose through the ranks of the merchant navy to become master of several ships. Given a commission as lieuten-ant in the U. S. Navy in 1798, he served in the Quasi-War with France and the Barbary Wars and would later command the frigates *Chesapeake, President* and in 1810, the *Constitution.* During the War of 1812, on the *Constitution* he was involved in a long sea chase, out running blockading British ships and taking the ship safely into Boston Harbor where he was given a huge reception and high praise in the press.

In the British press, on the other hand, Hull and his ship were treated with distain. They referred to the *Constitution* as, "a bundle of pine boards sailing under a bit of striped bunting" and went on to say that, "a few broadsides from England's wooden hulls will drive the paltry striped bunting from the ocean". On August 19, 1812, they were made to eat those words as the Constitution under the command of Commodore Hull met and destroyed the British frigate *Guerriere,* demonstrating the strength of the American frigate and Hull's seamanship. The Constitution suffered very little damage as her hull was made not of pine, but stout oak which earned her the nickname, "Old Ironsides". This battle greatly raised the morale of the American people and must have been very satisfying to Hull.

Isaac Hull captured several other British ships and after the war served as Commander of the Washington Navy Yard and later as commander of the Navy's Pacific Squadron. He died in 1843.

Five U.S. Navy ships have been named for him as well as many streets and the bridge across the Housatonic River in Connecticut.

MCDONOUGH STREET

Commodore Thomas McDonough
By Gilbert Stuart

"Down to the Civil War, he was the greatest figure in our naval history."

Just south of Hull Street and also laid out in 1801, this street was originally named Screven Street in honor of Brigadier General Screven who died at the Battle of Midway, Georgia in 1778 after being wounded three times by the British. It was renamed in 1815 for Commodore Thomas McDonough the naval hero who defeated the British on Lake Champlain in the War of 1812. Screven was later honored by having a county in Georgia named for him as well as the fort built on Tybee Island in 1899, during the Spanish-American War.

While the street in Savannah was named McDonough, as a teenager he changed the spelling of his name to Macdonough. Streets and towns named after him have used both spellings and to add to the confusion, sometimes even MacDonough.

Thomas McDonough was born in Odessa, Delaware in 1783. His father, a physician, joined the American forces and became a hero in the Revolutionary War. After his brother, a sailor, lost a leg in the Quasi War against the French, Thomas applied for a commission in the Navy and joined in 1800 as a midshipman aboard the *Constellation*, sister ship to the *Constitution*. He later served under Stephen Decatur in the Barbary Wars, playing a significant role in burning the captured *Philadelphia* which was aground in Tripoli Harbor. McDonough served as commander of several ships and when the War of 1812 began he was given the rank of Master Commander. In October of 1812, the newly promoted officer was assigned to Burlington, Vermont to command the American Naval "forces" on Lake Champlain. Those "forces" consisted of 2 small ships which because of the "impetuosity" of junior officers were captured giving control of the lake to British naval forces.

McDonough had to essentially start from scratch to construct a new fleet. During the winter of 1813-14, ice covered the lake giving the Americans time to build a corvette, a sloop and several gunboats at a shipyard in Vergennes, Vermont, and to convert a ferry into a seventeen gun warship. The British, too, were building ships and in May 1814 their fleet sailed down the Lake, anchored off shore and began to bombard the Americans. McDonough was prepared and the British were driven off allowing the small American fleet to sail to Plattsburgh, New York to prepare for a major British attack by land and sea.

The commander of the British army had delayed his attack on Plattsburg to allow time for the British fleet to neutralize American ships, but McDonough destroyed or captured most of their larger ships and the British army retreated to Canada. This victory meant that the British could not claim any American territory at the Peace conference in Ghent later that year.

For his role in this victory, McDonough was promoted to captain, presented with a Congressional Gold Medal and given land in both New York State and Vermont. As the rank of commodore did not come into existence until the Civil War, it was used during this period as a sign of respect. In his book, "The Naval War of 1812", Theodore Roosevelt wrote of McDonough, "Down to the Civil War, he was the greatest figure in our naval history".

After the war, McDonough returned to sea, commanding several ships including the *Constitution*. Suffering from tuberculosis, the Commodore took the *Constitution* on a cruise to the Mediterranean, but was overcome by his illness and had to relinquish command and attempt to return home. He died during that voyage on November 10, 1825.

Along with the street in Savannah, several towns including one in Georgia and his home town, Odessa, which was renamed for him, bear the name of McDonough. Four U.S. Navy destroyers have carried his name as well as a hall at the U.S. Naval Academy, a highway in New York State and an annual sailboat race on Lake Champlain. In 1937, his name and portrait appeared on a U. S. postage stamp.

PERRY STREET

Oliver Hazard Perry transferring from his stricken flagship, the Lawrence to the Niagara during the Battle of Lake Erie
By William Henry Powell

"We have met the enemy and they are ours..."

This third street laid out in 1801 and the third named for a naval hero of the War of 1812, was originally named Wilkes Street for John Wilkes (1785-1819) a Member of Parliament who had been a strong supporter of the Georgia colonists and a staunch defender of human rights. Because of his ridiculing of King George III and various prime ministers, he was not popular with fellow MPs and despite being described as the ugliest member in Parliament, Wilkes was a serial womanizer and a member of the Hellfire Club. He wrote a very pornographic poem entitled, "An Essay on Woman", which an enemy read out publically while Wilkes was recovering from a wound incurred in a duel. Wilkes was forced to flee to France when fellow members demanded his arrest, but he returned four years later and was reelected to

Parliament. It is up to the reader to look up a copy of "An Essay on Woman".

Perry Street, a west to east street just south of McDonough Street, was renamed in 1815 to honor yet another naval hero of the War of 1812. Oliver Hazard Perry was born in 1785 in South Kingston, Rhode Island, the son of a navy Captain and the older brother of Commodore Matthew Perry who is credited with the opening up of Japan. Appointed as a midshipman at the age of thirteen, he rose through the ranks to captain several U.S. navy ships.

At the beginning of the War of 1812, the British controlled most of the Great Lakes thus threatening the north western States.

Perry at his request was given command of the American fleet on Lake Erie; a fleet that was at that time still under construction at Put-in-Bay, Pennsylvania. *On September 10, 1813, the British* fleet appeared off Put-in-Bay and Perry took his now completed and armed fleet of nine ships out to meet them. Though outnumbered the British early on had the advantage and Perry's flagship, the *Lawrence* was badly damaged and captured. Perry was rowed half a mile through heavy gunfire to the *Niagara* and taking control of his fleet from there, so severely damaged the British ships that they were forced to capitulate.

He accepted the British surrender on the deck of the recaptured *Lawrence*. His report to General William Henry Harrison has become part of the tradition of the US Navy, "We have met the enemy and they are ours...".

Although this battle was relatively small, the victory was important as it allowed the American forces to recapture Detroit and Amherstburg and rout the British army and its Native

American allies at the battle of the Thames and provide protection for the entire Ohio Valley. Oliver Perry would be involved in nine other victorious battles following his success on Lake Erie. For his outstanding service during the war, Perry was awarded the Congressional Gold Medal and the Thanks of Congress and was promoted to captain, later, as with Isaac Hull and Thomas McDonough, came the promotion to Commodore.

Following the war, Captain Perry commanded the frigate *Java* during the Second Barbary War and in 1819 was sent on an expedition to Venezuela to discuss the problem of piracy in the Caribbean with Simon Bolivar, where he contracted yellow fever and died on his birthday. He was buried in Port of Spain, but his remains were later returned to Newport, Rhode Island and buried in the Island Cemetery.

There are many towns, villages and counties including Perry, Georgia, named for Commodore Perry as well as a number of monuments in many States and one in Trinidad. Seven US Navy ships have borne his name as well as the Rhode Island Educational Foundation tall ship, the SSV Oliver Hazard Perry.

LIBERTY STREET

"Woods with only a few scattered houses, the Poor House, the Negro cemetery, overgrown wartime defenses and a variety of wild animals"

Liberty Street was the fourth west to east street laid out and named by the Savannah City Council in 1801 and the only one of the four that didn't have its name changed later. This wide sandy thoroughfare was given the name Liberty to celebrate America winning its independence from the British in the Revolutionary War. According to an article in the Georgia

Historical Quarterly, at the time of its creation the area to the south was,

> *grasslands leading to woods with only a few scattered houses, the Poor House, the Negro Cemetery, overgrown wartime defenses and a variety of wild animals.*

In 1837 an ordinance was passed to widen the street to 130 feet. A median was added and planted with scrubs and trees.

One of the main features of this street was the construction of the Oglethorpe barracks completed in 1834. Used originally by the United States Army for among, other things the conducting of meteorological observations. Confederate troops were stationed there during the Civil War and it was again occupied by federal troops at the end of that war. Decommissioned in 1879 and sold to the Savannah Hotel Corporation, the barracks were torn down to make way for the construction of the Desoto Hotel, a Savannah landmark for many years.

The original Desoto Hotel with the monument to Sgt. Jasper in the foreground

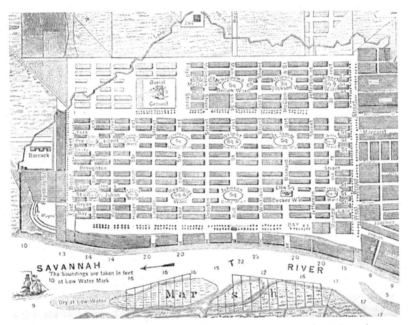

Map of Savannah drawn and published in 1818 by I Stouf

Courtesy of the Hargrett Rare Book and Manuscript Library, University of
Georgia

HARRIS STREET

"...we have lost an honest man and a good member of society."
Harris Street, created in those grasslands south of Liberty Street, was named for Francis Harris* who with James Habersham opened the first commercial house in the Colony of Georgia. An ordinance of the Savannah City Council of March 28, 1837, laid out and named this west to east street.

Harris arrived in the colony in about 1739, a couple of years after Habersham, but neither originally showed any promise of becoming leaders; Harris becoming a clerk in the trustees' store and Habersham a school master. However, the two created the firm of Harris and Habersham in 1744 and began purchasing supplies in Charleston to sell in Savannah. They encouraged local farmers and producers to begin thinking of producing not just enough to fill the needs of local residents, but also a surplus to sell abroad.

After establishing contacts with a commercial house in London, the firm chartered a small ship, loaded it with rice, staves, tar, pitch and deer skins and sent it off to England. This was the first ship chartered to a company in the colony and it was soon followed by others taking cargoes not only to London, but to Boston, Philadelphia and New York as well. This trade made both Harris and Habersham wealthy men, but also added to the wealth of other colonists and brought in goods and luxuries previously unobtainable to Georgians.

Their commercial prosperity also brought about political success. During the last years of the Trusteeship, Harris and Habersham assumed the major responsibility for handling the Trustees' business affairs in Georgia and both were appointed as assistants to President Stephens, thus having considerable say in the allocation of land grants. Harris was named Speaker of Georgia's first General Assembly in 1751 and was made a member of the Royal Council.

In the mid 1750's after ten years in the import-export business both men retired to become rice planters. Francis Harris had been granted 1300 acres in 1762 and purchased 1600 additional acres in the same area on the Little Ogeechee River which included a house built several years earlier. The House and plantation were named "Wild Heron" after an estate in England once owned by his wife, Mary. By 1769, Harris had accrued considerable holdings, but Mary died in 1770 and Francis a year later. Their son, Francis Henry Harris inherited the plantation, but was later killed fighting the British during the Revolutionary War.

Wild Heron Plantation

When Francis Harris died, James Habersham wrote, "You will join me that we have lost an honest man and a good member of society."

* Thomas Gamble, former mayor of Savannah, wrote in his *A History of City government of Savannah, Georgia from 1790 to 1901 that* Harris Street was named for Charles Harris, mayor of the city from 1802 to 1804, but the street was named in 1801 before Charles Harris took office and grew to prominence some years later.

TATTNALL STREET

Bonaventure Cemetery

"...an honest man. Rich in the estimation of all who knew him."

Perhaps the shortest street in the Historic District, running north to south from just Liberty Street to Hall Street, Tattnall Street was named for Josiah Tattnall Jr. Born in 1762, in Beaufort, South Carolina, Tattnall moved to Savannah with his family as a child and lived on Bonaventure Plantation which was owned jointly by his father and John Mulryne.

When the struggle for American independence began both Josiah Tattnall Sr. and John Mulryne remained staunchly loyal to the King. In 1776, the two were, with a number of other loyalists, condemned for "high treason" by the new independent assembly, forced to flee, and their property confiscated and resold.

Young Josiah Tattnall Jr. however, had a strong attachment to Georgia and there is the story that as the ship taking his family away from Savannah sailed, he jumped overboard and attempted to swim back ashore. He was caught, brought back aboard and the family sailed first to the Bahamas and then to England.

Josiah was enrolled at Eton College, but problems caused by his restlessness and longing to return to Georgia led to his father having him enlisted in the Royal Navy. In 1782, he was assigned to a ship headed for America. Josiah jumped ship in the first American port, made his way to Savannah and joined the Continental army under General "Mad Anthony" Wayne, which was confronting the British at Savannah. Unfortunately he arrived as the war was ending and was unable to do more than show his willingness to serve his State.

Tattnall continued his military career after the war, joining the Georgia Militia under General James Jackson and participating in the putting down of a slave rebellion in 1787 and Native American uprisings in 1788 and 1793. He was made captain of the Chatham Artillery and later colonel of an infantry regiment. Several years before his death Tattnall was promoted to Brigadier General.

Politically, Tattnall was also successful, being elected to the Georgia House of Representatives in 1795. During his term, he campaigned to win votes to rescind the Yazoo Land Act which allowed corrupt officials to influence the sale of millions of acres of State land. He served in the Georgia Senate from 1796 to 1799 and was elected governor in 1801, serving only one year during which The University of Georgia was chartered and the State's northern and western boundaries were established.

In 1788, Tattnall bought part of the Bonaventure Plantation, given up by his father a number of years earlier. Unfortunately for him and his wife, Harriet, the plantation did not live up to its name and within five years both would be buried there.

There is the story that while the couple were hosting a Christmas dinner for many notables, a servant came in and quietly whispered something to Josiah. He got up and calmly announced that since the weather was so pleasant, the party would be moved outside on to the lawn. The table and chairs were duly moved and the dinner continued in the light of the blaze which was consuming the house. It is said that toasts were made to the family and to the house and then the crystal glasses were thrown against a nearby oak tree.

Josiah Tattnall Jr. died in 1803 at the age of 38 in the Bahamas, where he had gone in an attempt to improve his health. His body was returned to Savannah and buried next to his wife who had died the year before. The inscription on his tomb reads in part, "…an honest man. Rich in the estimation of all who knew him." Tattnall County in Georgia was named for him and a Liberty ship built at the Southeastern Shipbuilding Corporation during World War II also bore his name. Bonaventure Plantation became a privately owned cemetery in 1846 and has been operated as a public cemetery by the City of Savannah since 1907.

RIVER STREET

The bluff before the construction of wharves and River Street

This is another puzzling bit of Savannah history. When was the road along the river which would eventually become River Street, actually constructed? Initially, small ships would come right up to the bluff to unload while the larger vessels would offload onto small boats. All cargo was hauled up or lowered by a crane. Eleven years after the colony was established, Francis Harris and James Habersham constructed an "unpretentious place of business" under the bluff by the water's edge. In 1759, the first wharf was built below the crane on the bluff between Whitaker and Bull Streets.

As the town grew, additional wharves were constructed and merchants conducted business on those wharves or directly onboard the ships. Importing and exporting increased rapidly and between 1790 and 1840 warehouses were built starting at river level and then rising to a height of six floors in order to be higher than the bluff. Factors, those who brokered the sale of goods, used the upper floors as their offices while merchandise was warehoused below. There was a space between the south side of these buildings and the bluff and the bluff had to be shored up with stone in 1840. Iron bridges were then constructed from the bluff to the buildings, creating Factor's Walk.

When, then, was River Street constructed? Thomas Gamble in his *History of the City Government of Savannah, Georgia From 1790 to 1901,* wrote that there was mention of the street in city council minutes in 1829 regarding whether a portion of the street was public domain or private property. The street may have been laid out earlier, but by 1829, it was commonly being referred to as River Street. The earliest map showing the name River Street appeared in 1845.

The street and the businesses along it thrived for several decades. Rice, then cotton, lumber and naval stores were shipped to the North and all over Europe, however, the boll weevil destroyed the cotton trade and later, after World War II, the harbor moved upriver. The street and the warehouses fell into a state of serious disrepair which lasted until the early 1970's.

River Street in 1970
Courtesy Georgia Global Design News

With funds from several U.S. government agencies and from

the City of Savannah, the River Street Urban Renewal Project was completed in 1977 transforming the derelict area into a major attraction for the city. Trendy shops, pubs, restaurants and hotels are now housed in buildings where cotton was once stored, major events like the monthly First Saturday, St. Patrick's Day and the Fourth of July are elaborately celebrated, all attracting more than a million tourists and revelers every year.

River Street today
Photo courtesy Savannah Waterfront Association

Many monuments relating to Savannah's past, line River Street as well. The African American Monument, The Waving Girl, the 1966 Olympic Yachting Caldron, The World War II Monument and the Anchor Monument honoring Merchant Mariners lost at sea are among those found on this exciting street.

The Waving Girl
Courtesy of the Georgia Department of Economic Development

MACON STREET

Nathaniel Macon

Portrait by Robert D. Gauley for the U.S. House of Representatives in 1911.
(Macon refused to have his portrait painted while he was alive.)

Macon was for thirty seven years the most prominent nay-sayer in Congress.

In 1839, the Savannah City council passed an ordinance extending the city limits southward by creating three new west to east streets. Macon Street was named for a man who was not a Georgian and had no connections to the State, but who was beloved by Georgians because of his States' Rights ideology.

Nathaniel Macon was born in North Carolina in 1758, was educated in a rustic school in what is today Warren County, and attended the College of New Jersey (Princeton University). Clues as to his character became evident early on when he left school to join the New Jersey Militia at the beginning of the Revolutionary War. He joined as a private refusing election to a lieutenancy and the $150 enlistment bounty.

Returning to North Carolina after the war, he was elected without running to the State Senate. This, too would become a pattern. His political career included 28 years in the U.S. House of Representatives and almost a decade in the U.S. Senate, and not once did he put himself forward or actually run for office. He later claimed that, "I never solicited any man to vote for me or hinted at him that I wished him to do so." He turned down many offers to run for office including that of John Quincy Adams as his vice presidential running mate. He never abused the power of any office, never maximized an expense account and never asked for a public position for a relative.

Macon was an ardent anti-federalist and extremely pro States' Rights, wary of a strong federal government that strayed from the provisions of the Constitution. During his entire term in Congress he cast more negative votes than any other ten members combined. Perhaps the only time that Nathaniel Macon's honesty was tested and he failed was during his courtship of Hannah Plummer. He challenged another suiter to a card game with Hannah as the prize. Macon lost, but reneged on the bet saying to Hannah, "notwithstanding I have lost you fairly...love is superior to honesty...I cannot give you up". They were married on October 9, 1783, but Hannah lived only seven more years followed in death by their only son a year later. Nathaniel lived for forty-seven more years, dying in 1837. He never remarried.

Not only did he refuse to have his portrait painted, but he also burned most of his papers and had threatened to sue anyone intending to write his biography. His quest to insure his oblivion in life, however, was not honored after his death. Several biographies were written, Macon County and the City of Macon in Georgia along with many places in North Carolina and several other States were named for him as well as Randolph Macon University in Virginia.

The City of Savannah in 1837
By Fermin Cerveau

CHARLTON STREET

The Steamship Savannah, The first steamship to cross the Atlantic Ocean

Joined President Monroe on the shakedown cruise of the Steamship Savannah

This gentleman must have had one of the most exciting experiences any Savannahian of the day could have had. The second of three streets created in 1839, Charlton Street was named for Thomas Usher Pulaski Charlton. Running west to east just south of Macon Street, Charlton Street was for a brief period the southern boundary of the city.

Thomas U. P. Charlton was born into a prominent family in Camden, South Carolina in 1779. His father, a surgeon who served in the American army during the Revolutionary War and later as a member of the South Carolina legislature, died in 1789 and his mother moved with her son to Savannah in 1791. Thomas was sent to school at St. John's College in Maryland where he was joined by his first cousin, Francis Scott Key who wrote the lyrics for the Star Spangled Banner. The two would become lifelong correspondents.

Charlton was admitted to the State Bar at the age of twenty and quickly gained a reputation as an excellent lawyer. Just four years later, Governor John Milledge appointed him to the position of Attorney General for the State of Georgia, a position which allowed him to become experienced in the field of criminal justice.

In 1807, he was elected judge of the Eastern Circuit of Georgia, serving in that capacity until 1811, and using his position to urge grand juries to bring about reforms to the State and national penal systems. He wrote that, "The sanguinary code of Great Britain which is in part still sanctioned in this State is incompatible with the enlightened and mild principles of the American Government".

Thomas Charlton was a Democratic Republican, an ardent anti-Federalist and a strong supporter of Thomas Jefferson. In a letter written in March 1801 congratulating the new president on his elevation to that office, he wrote,

It was time, Sir, that the rights of freemen of America should be rescued from the grasp of domestic usurpation; and the idea is fondly cherished, that the influence of your experience—your wisdom, combined with the energies of a regenerated legislature, may…bring back our institutions to their original purity.

Such high praise did not result three years later in a sought after appointment to the post of U.S. District Attorney in New Orleans.

Charlton was strongly opposed to dueling, considering this activity "barbaric, nonsensible and repulsive". This is ironic as one of his closest friends was James Jackson, who reportedly fought twenty-three duels, earning for himself the title of "The

Brawling Pigmy" and an early grave because of his many wounds.

Thomas, who with the rank of major had served as Jackson's aide-de-camp during peacetime, published a biography of the general entitled, *The Life of Major General James Jackson,* in 1809.

During the War of 1812, Charlton served as chairman of the Committee of Public Safety and in 1815 was elected mayor by the city council. Throughout the first of six terms in that position he would be praised for his leadership through a major fire and a yellow fever epidemic. On May 11, 1819, during an interval between his many terms as mayor, Charlton was invited along with other local dignitaries to join President James Monroe for a cruise down the Savannah River on the steamship *Savannah* which only a few days later would begin its epic voyage to become the first steamship to cross the Atlantic Ocean.

Thomas Charlton was involved with a number of civic organizations including being a founding member of the Hibernian Society and Worthy Grand Master of the Masons. He was married four times, the first three wives dying at a relatively young age. One of his sons, Robert Milledge Charlton also became a noted jurist in Savannah. Thomas died of a fever at the age of fifty-six on December 14, 1835 and was buried in Colonial Cemetery. His body was later moved to the family plot in Laurel Grove Cemetery.

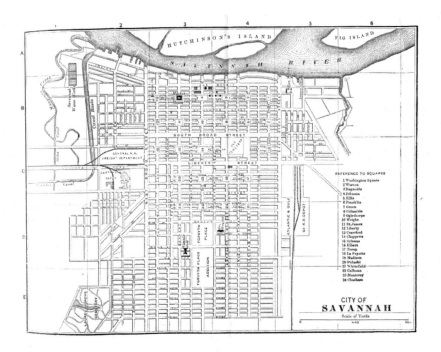

Map of the City of Savannah published in 1856 by John M. Cooper

Courtesy of the Hargrett Rare Book and Manuscript Library, University of Georgia

JONES STREET

"But pray do not be unhappy on my account, and believe that if it is my fate to survive this action, I shall: if otherwise, the Lord's will be done."

American attack on British held Savannah, October 9, 1779
By A. I. Keller

Many native Savannahians believe that Jones Street was named for Noble Jones, one of the original Georgia colonists, leading colonial official, friend of General Oglethorpe and proprietor of Wormsloe Plantation. Possibly others still might consider that his son, Noble Wimberley Jones, a physician and Revolutionary War hero, is the street's namesake. Both would be good assumptions, but we all know about assumptions. The "Savannah Georgian" newspaper ran a story on March 15, 1839, indicating that the street was in fact named for Major John Jones killed during the American attempt to retake Savannah from the British during the Revolutionary War.

The new street is to be called Jones Street, it may be worthy of remark, as a compliment to the father of Captain John Jones of Liberty County, who fell within one hundred yards of the spot patriotically dedicated to his name while fighting for the liberties of his country. Thus has posterity been grateful to one of its deliverers from foreign thralldom.

Jones Street was the third street laid out in 1839 and ran west to east just south of Charlton Street. For just two years it would constitute the city's southern boundary.

John Jones was born in South Carolina in 1749 and as an adult moved to Georgia where he purchased land in what is now the lower part of Liberty County. He resided at Sunbury in the summer and on his rice plantation called Rice Hope during the winter months. He was also an importing merchant.

As did most Georgians of the period, Jones served in the military, participating in the Cherokee Wars, 1769-71, and when the American struggle for independence began in 1775 he volunteered to serve once again. During the Siege of Savannah in late 1779, Jones, now a major, was made aide-de-camp to General Lachlan McIntosh. On September 29, he was ordered to meet with the British commander, General Prevost under a flag of truce to request that women and children in the city including General McIntosh's family be allowed to leave before the Americans began their bombardment. Jones found McIntosh's wife and children huddled in a damp cellar, but the British commander refused the request.

In the early hours of October 4th, that bombardment began and later in the day Jones wrote a letter to his wife stating that,

Last night at twelve o'clock, we began to open our bomb battery

and this morning at five o'clock we began with our battering cannon—a sight that I would not miss seeing. We are still at it. And I do not expect that we shall cease for forty-eight hours. At the end of that time I hope that Savannah will have surrendered...I heartily desire to see the day when I inform you of our success. But pray do not be unhappy on my account, and believe that if it is my fate to survive this action, I shall: if otherwise, the Lord's will must be done.

Five days later, on October 9, 1779, he was cut in half by a cannonball while leading the forlorn hope (basically a unit selected for a suicide charge) in an attempt to storm a British battery at Spring Hill, located just one hundred yards from the beginning of the street that would later be constructed and given his name. He died seven weeks before the birth of his youngest son, Joseph, who would command the Liberty County Independent troops in the War of 1812. He is buried in Midway Cemetery. Major John Jones was also an ancestor of Charles Colcock Jones, historian and Mayor of Savannah in 1860.

TAYLOR STREET

General Zachary Taylor
Official White House portrait by Joseph Henry Bush 1848

"He died of a combination of official scandals, Washington heat and doctors"

In 1847, four more west to east streets were constructed extending Savannah's boundary further south. The first, Taylor Street, was named for Zachary Taylor a general who led American troops in the Mexican War and later became the twelfth President of the United States. Born on a plantation in Orange County, Virginia he moved with his family to Kentucky during his youth.

Taylor was commissioned a lieutenant in the army in 1808 and promoted to captain two years later. He was involved in a number of battles in the War of 1812 and after the war supervised the construction of a number of forts in Louisiana. He eventually bought a plantation and moved his wife Margaret and their children to that State. At the age of seventeen, his eldest daughter, Sarah, married the young lieutenant, Jefferson

Davis who would later become president of the Confederacy. Although Taylor respected Davis, he disapproved of the marriage because he didn't want his daughter to become an army wife.

Zachary Taylor was promoted several times while fighting in the Indian Wars and after winning a major battle against the Seminoles at Lake Okeechobee on Christmas Day 1837, was promoted to brigadier general. During the Mexican War, he defeated a much larger Mexican Army at Palo Alto and Resaca de la Palma, captured the City of Monterey and overcame General Santa Anna's army at Buena Vista, earning promotion to major general. During his military career he earned the nickname of "Old Rough and Ready", in part because of his lack of care with his uniforms.

His successes began to be noticed in Washington and some thought that he would be a strong candidate for the presidency even though no one was quite sure of his political views. Though he owned slaves, he was not in favor of expanding slavery and was staunchly opposed to secession. In response to a question about being interested in running, he replied, "Such an idea never entered my head...nor is it likely to enter the head of any sane person". Interested or not, he received the Whig party nomination, was elected and took office in January 1849, becoming the last slave owning president. The outgoing president, James K. Polk, was not impressed with Taylor, saying that he was, "without political information" and "wholly unqualified for the station".

In office, President Taylor's main goal was the preservation of the Union, but his few months in office were in general undistinguished. At a celebration on July 4, 1850, a particularly hot day, after eating raw fruit and drinking iced milk, he became ill with acute gastroenteritis and despite or perhaps because of his treatment died five days later. Samuel Eliot Morrison in his *Oxford History of the American People* wrote, "He died of a combination of official scandals, Washington heat and doctors."

President Zachary Taylor has been honored with his image on postage stamps, with many places including Taylor County, Georgia and a World War II Liberty ship named for him.

WAYNE STREET

James Moore Wayne
Portrait by John Maier

"He was a sincere and honest patriot. Let us constantly follow his example."

Wayne Street was unusual in that it was created in 1851, between Taylor and Gordon Streets, both laid out four years earlier. It was named for James Moore Wayne, the first Georgia appointee to the U. S. Supreme Court. Born in Savannah in 1790, Wayne graduated from The College of New Jersey (Princeton University), studied law in New Haven Connecticut, was admitted to the Bar in 1810 and began practicing in Savannah. During the War of 1812, he served as an officer in the Georgia Hussars. He was elected to the Georgia House of Representatives in 1815 and, following in his father's footsteps, was Mayor of Savannah from 1817 to 1819.

Wayne's judicial career began in 1820, as judge of the Court of Common Pleas and then judge of the Superior Court of Savannah from 1822 to 1828. He was elected to U. S. Congress in

1829 resigning in 1835 to accept an appointment by President Andrew Jackson to the U. S. Supreme Court, a post he held until his death in Washington in 1867.

Judge Wayne was opposed to slavery, but thought that it had to be tolerated to preserve the Union. He favored a strong federal government believing that a citizen's loyalty belonged first to the nation then to his region and finally to his State. This was not a popular position in the South and when Georgia seceded, Wayne remained on the bench even though other southern judges resigned. Taking such an unpopular position resulted in a trial in a Confederate Court where he was deemed an "alien" in Georgia and deprived of his lands. The lands were never actually confiscated being given instead to his son, a general in the Confederate Army.

The house designed by William Jay that Judge Wayne had had built on the corner of Oglethorpe Avenue and Bull Street was sold in 1831 to William Washington Gordon, the grandfather of Juliette Gordon Low, the founder of the Girl Scouts of America. There was also a family connection as Wayne's sister was the great-grandmother of Juliette Gordon Low. The house today is revered by Girl Scouts all over America as the birthplace of the founder of that movement.

In spite of being branded an alien during the war, upon his death Judge Wayne's body was returned to Savannah and buried in Laurel Grove Cemetery.

GORDON STREET

William Washington Gordon monument in Wright Square

"Ten cheers for the railroad and Gordon."

Wayne and Gordon Streets, are not just in close physical proximity, the two men for whom they were named were also close. William Washington Gordon read Law under Judge James Moore Wayne and later bought the house that Wayne had built (which eventually became the Juliette Gordon Low House). As mentioned previously, Judge Wayne's sister was also Juliette Gordon Low's great grandmother and in 1826 his niece, Sarah Stites, would marry Gordon.

William Washington Gordon was born in Screven County, Georgia in 1796 and when his father died he was sent to school in Rhode Island and then to West Point, where he became the first Georgian to graduate from that institution. He served in the army for less than a year before moving to Savannah to study Law under Judge Wayne. Gordon became a member of the Bar in 1820 and was elected mayor of Savannah 1834. He then served several terms in the Georgia General Assembly.

Gordon's greatest contribution to the City and the State was the creation of the Central Railroad and Banking Company, later the Central of Georgia Railroad. Savannah's port was in serious danger of being crippled because of the difficulty of getting cotton from the interior of the State to Savannah. The Port of Charleston already had a railroad giving it that capability and had basically cornered the market.

Gordon was consumed by the quest for this railroad and abandoning his law practice and resigning from his position as mayor, devoted all of his time to the planning and the raising of funds for the project. Construction began in 1836 and by 1839 seventy-six miles of tract had been laid in the direction of Macon, Georgia. Much to his wife's dismay, Gordon traveled constantly, supervising construction, negotiating rights of way and dealing with labor problems.

The line reached Macon in 1843, but Gordon was not there to see the last spike being driven. He died at home on March 22, 1842, of bilious pleurisy. That his efforts on behalf of the City were appreciated is illustrated by a letter to him from his wife, Sarah, describing a celebration in Savannah in 1835: "A band came around the house at about ten o'clock yelling 'Ten Cheers for the railroad and Gordon". William Washington Gordon was buried in Colonial Cemetery, but was later reinterred at Laurel Grove.

Along with the street in Savannah, Gordon County, Georgia is also named for him. Unfortunately, after his death, several actions were taken in his name which were unpopular with the remaining members of the Creek Tribe in Georgia. In 1843, a year after his death, the railroad built a rail line through the site of The Ocmulgee National Monument near Macon, desecrating that important Native American site. In 1873, a second line was constructed partially destroying the Funeral Mound, the burial site of the ancestors of the Creek Indians and to add further insult to that desecration, workers carried off the bones and artifacts.

Not done with the destroying of its relationship with the Creeks, in 1882, the Central of Georgia Railway Company decided to construct a forty-seven foot tall granite and marble memorial to Gordon in the middle of Wright Square. Unfortunately, that meant destroying the grave of Tomochichi, the Chief of the tribe that had greeted General Oglethorpe and the first colonists and provided land and advice for them as they endeavored to establish the colony.

(The interesting story of the construction of the new monument for the Mico can be found under his name in Appendix A.)

Savannah in 1889

GASTON STREET

William Gaston's tomb (The Stranger's Tomb) in Bonaventure Cemetery

"Savannah's host to the living and the dead."

The fourth street created by the City Council in 1847 was named for William Gaston who was born in 1785 in Somerset County, New Jersey. He moved to Savannah in 1805 and established himself as a cotton merchant, later becoming director and then president of the Planter's Bank in the building now known as The Olde Pink House.

Gaston never married, but became well known for giving lavish parties for dignitaries from around the world. Mayor Thomas Gamble would later call him, "The Prince of Savannah". It was, however, not just dignitaries that Gaston would welcome; he also befriended strangers and poor visitors stranded in Savannah earning the sobriquet, "The Stranger's Friend".

John James Audubon was both a dignitary and a stranger when he arrived in Savannah in 1832 after an unsuccessful sales tour of Florida and having survived a major storm on the voyage to the city. Wanting to publicize his bird folios in the city, he met with an acquaintance who introduced him to Gaston. Gaston listened to Audubon as he described his work and was impressed. After buying a set himself, he said,

> *Every one of us is bound to you for the knowledge you bring to us which without your zeal and enterprise might probably never reached us. I will now make it my duty to serve you and will be your agent in this city.*

The Savannah merchant and banker was able to secure a number of sales of *Birds of America* from local residents at a price of $1000 per set, a phenomenal amount at the time. Audubon later wrote expressing his gratitude to the Savannahian who, "nobly resolved to exert himself in the cause of science." He went on to say, "I trust that he will not consider it improper of me to inform you, that on inquiring at Savannah for William Gaston, Esq., you will readily find him."

William Gaston died on a business trip to New York City in 1837 and in his will he stipulated that money be set aside to build a house of residence for "persons of color". That house was built later that year at 511 E. Congress Street and still exists today. Gaston was originally buried in Colonial Cemetery, but in 1873 his remains were moved to Bonaventure Cemetery and housed in a mausoleum paid for by public subscription. It contained space for Gaston and two others, for use by strangers who died while visiting Savannah until relatives could make permanent arrangements for their remains. In 1925, Mayor Thomas Gamble said of Gaston that he was, "Savannah's host to the living and the dead".

HUNTINGDON STREET

Selina Hastings, Countess of Huntingdon
Portrait by Unknown Artist

"All aflame for Jesus"

Selina Hastings, Countess of Huntingdon was a distant cousin of George Washington, but that's not why the street just south of Gaston Street was named for her in 1851. Rather, it was because of her association with and assistance to George Whitefield and John and Charles Wesley in their apostolic works in the Colony of Georgia.

Born Lady Selina Shirley in 1707 in Leicestershire, England, into a wealthy and titled family, her childhood was spent between Leicestershire and her father's Irish estates. In 1728, she married Theophilus Hastings, 9th Earl of Huntingdon, (that title, the Earl of Huntingdon, being the same as that given to the legendary folk hero Robin Hood several centuries earlier). A series of serious illnesses were probably the cause of the Countess converting to Methodism in 1739 and joining John Wesley's Methodist Society in Fetter's Lane, London. Later, she developed an appreciation for the preaching of George Whitefield and when there arose a split between the Wesleys and Whitefield which she tried to reconcile, her relationship with the Wesleys became strained.

In 1747, the Countess's husband died and she devoted her wealth, her status, indeed her life to her religion. She funded sixty chapels, appointed their preachers and created a college to train preachers. This network of her own sect of Calvinistic Methodism became known as "The Countess of Huntingdon's Connexion", leading Whitefield to describe her as a "Methodist Archbishop". It is estimated that she gave the equivalent of many millions in today's dollars to the funding of the gospel earning her another title as "Lady Bountiful". Horace Walpole described her as the "patriarchtress of the Methodists" and George Whitefield wrote that she was "All aflame for Jesus".

It would be Whitefield who would involve her in Bethesda the first orphanage in the colonies. Whitefield had come to the Colony of Georgia in 1738 and saw the need for an orphanage. He sought funding for his project throughout the colonies and from friends in England, one of whom was the Countess, a longtime supporter of his ministry. When he died in 1770, his will stated that

> *I will and bequeath the orphan house in Bethesda and likewise all buildings, land. Books and furniture belonging thereto, to that lady elect, that mother of Israel, that mirror of fine and undefiled religion, the Right Honorable Selina, Countess of Huntingdon.*

The Countess did provide financial support, but in 1773, much of the orphanage burned to the ground and although she vowed to rebuild it, her efforts were stymied by illness and the beginning of the American Revolution. Bethesda was later rebuilt and operated for many years by the Union Society. While no longer an orphanage, it still exists today as the Bethesda Academy, a member of the Coalition for Residential Education.

Selina, Countess of Huntingdon continued her support for the Methodist movement until her death in 1791. It is said that her last words were, "My work is done; I have nothing to do but go to my Father". As well as the street in Savannah, a county in Pennsylvania and a university in Alabama have been named for her.

View of Savannah published in 1872
By Henry Fenn

HALL STREET

"I resume my Pen to confirm what you have no Doubt heard, that our worthy Friend Gwinnett has unfortunately fell."

Hall Street named in 1851 for Lyman Hall, one of the three Georgia signers of the Declaration of independence, is the penultimate west to east Street in the Historic District.

Lyman Hall was born into a wealthy family in Connecticut in 1724, and graduated from Yale in 1747. After continued studies in theology, he began to preach in Bridgeport. In 1751, following charges of immoral conduct, which were proven and to which he confessed, he was dismissed from his church. However, he convinced church leaders that he was sincerely repentant and was subsequently allowed to return to the ministry. Only two years later, however, he chose to give up the ministry, began studying medicine and later received the degree of Doctor of Medicine. His first wife died after just one year of marriage and he then married Mary Osborn. Hall then took his wife and son to

South Carolina to join a Congregationalist settlement on the Ashley River near Charleston. The move proved to be a happy one and professionally successful.

The group began to look at the vast unsettled areas of the new Colony of Georgia as a means of ensuring future prosperity and after obtaining a grant of over 22,000 acres, began to immigrate to St. John's Parish in what is today Liberty County. The Hall family followed in 1756, purchasing a small plantation and then two lots in Sunbury where he built a summer residence.

Hall soon became the leading physician in the area and was described as "being six feet tall, well proportioned, cultured and educated, had polite manners and was of a well-rounded character".

As the relationship between the Colonies and England became more and more strained, Hall, became, as did most of the residents in the Midway/Sunbury area, a staunch advocate of independence. He attended meetings of "The Friends of Liberty" in Savannah where he became close friends with Button Gwinnett. Many in Savannah still had close ties with the mother country and Hall became frustrated with the inability of the Georgia's Colonial Assembly to take action.

When Georgia hesitated to send representatives to the Second Continental Congress in May 1775, Lyman Hall was elected to attend as a representative of the Parish of St. John. He was welcomed, but declined to vote on any matters which were to be decided by a vote of the colonies. The Colony of Georgia finally elected three members to the Congress, Button Gwinnett, George Walton and Lyman Hall and all three voted for independence and signed the Declaration on July 4, 1776.

Hall along with the other signers was now considered a traitor to the Crown and when the British captured Savannah and overran Liberty County, he had to flee with his family to Connecticut. His home and plantation were confiscated and burned, causing great financial loss. After Independence was won, Hall returned to the Savannah area in 1782 and resumed his medical practice. His reputation, gained both as a physician and political leader, led to his election as Governor of the new State in 1783. While he served just one one-year term, he dealt with a number of important issues including confiscated estates, frontier problems, and a seriously depleted treasury. His requests in 1785 to the legislature to grant tracts of land and endow institutions of learning led later to the chartering of the University of Georgia.

In 1790, Lyman Hall moved to Burke County, purchasing the Shell Bluff plantation on the Savannah River. He died there several months later and was buried in a substantial vault on the plantation. In 1848, his remains were moved to Augusta and interred under a monument to the Georgia signers in front of the courthouse. George Walton was also buried there, but Button Gwinnett was not and that's an interesting story which will follow.

Schools in Georgia and Connecticut were named for Hall as was Hall County in Georgia. The fifth Liberty ship launched at the Southeastern Shipbuilding Corporation in Savannah during World War II also bore his name.

GWINNETT STREET

Button Gwinnett
Portrait by Nathaniel Hone

Button Gwinnett

Button, Button whose got the Button?

Gwinnett Street, the last street in the designated National Historic District, was named for Button Gwinnett, one of the three Georgia signers of the Declaration of Independence. Laid out probably in 1851, it also forms the northern border of the National Victorian District.

You might think the name, Button, is another of those funny first names peculiar to the American South, but Button Gwinnett was born, in Gloucestershire, England in 1732, and Button was a family surname. Button Gwinnett was as a youth apprenticed to a merchant in Bristol where he later married, became an exporter of goods to the American Colonies and the owner of a brig. The business failed, however, and the ship was sold to pay debts. Debts would become the story of his life.

Seeking prosperity in a new setting, Gwinnett moved his

family to Charleston, South Carolina in the early 1760's and set himself up as a dry goods merchant there. Selling out several years later, he moved to Georgia and entered a similar business selling "Turlington's Elixir of Life", "Mr. James' Powders for Fever", cutlery, earthenware and tobacco. This, too, failed. Realizing that perhaps he was not cut out to be a businessman, he decided to become a planter, borrowed money from Thomas Bosomworth, the third husband of Mary Musgrove and bought St. Catherine's Island near Sunbury. There, he became acquainted with a group of settlers originally from Connecticut including Dr. Lyman Hall. It would be through his friendship with Hall that Gwinnett became interested in politics.

He was appointed justice of the peace in St. John's Parish and several years later was elected to the Georgia House of Commons. Chronic debts forced a withdrawal from politics and the sale of St. Catherine's. Ever ambitious, in 1776, Gwinnett became embroiled in a controversy over the leadership of the regiment of Georgia troops authorized by the Continental Congress. He wanted the position, but had no military experience and it was awarded to Lachlan McIntosh, an individual destined to become his nemesis.

Gwinnett instead was elected to be one of Georgia's members to the Continental Congress.

Prior to this election, Gwinnett had not shown any great sympathy for the Independence movement. His friend, Lyman Hall wrote that Gwinnett thought it foolhardy to take on a country as powerful as Britain. It would be Hall who persuaded him to change his views. He voted for independence on July 2nd and signed the Declaration of Independence on July 4, 1776.

Returning to the Georgia General Assembly later in 1776,

Gwinnett was elected speaker and played an important role in drafting Georgia's first constitution. When Governor Archibald Bulloch died in March of 1777, he was selected to fill that role becoming both governor and commander-in-chief of the army. The latter a position he was ill-equipped to hold and one which would ultimately lead to his demise. On taking office, Gwinnett immediately ordered the drafting of militia and volunteers for an attack on the British in East Florida even though the commanding general of the Continental Army in the South considered such an expedition to be too risky. The new governor ordered Colonel Lachlan McIntosh to lead the poorly planned expedition which failed miserably. The two rivals blamed each other for the failure. About this time, McIntosh's brother, George, became involved in a shaky business deal with two Royalists. Gwinnett found out and ordered that George be arrested, placed in irons and charged with treason. Gwinnett failed to be re-elected as governor and when the new assembly met to discuss the disastrous campaign in East Florida and exonerated Gwinnett, McIntosh became furious and called Gwinnett "a Scoundrel and a lying Rascal" to his face and in front of the assembly. Gwinnett demanded an apology or satisfaction. No apology was forthcoming and the date for a duel was set for May 16, 1777.

Button Gwinnett's friend, Dr. Lyman Hall described the event in a letter to Roger Sherman;

...they were placed at 10 or 12 feet distance. Discharged their pistols nearly at the same time. Each wounded in the thigh. Mr. Gwinnett's thigh broke so that he fell – on which (it is said) the Genl (general) Asked him if he chose to take a second shot – was answered Yes. If they could help him up...The seconds interposed and Mr.

Gwinnett was brought in, the Weather Extremely hot....A Mortification came on – he languish'd from that Morning (Friday) till Monday Morning following & expired.

Aftermath of the duel with Lachlan McIntosh

Hall was devastated by the death of his friend and demanded that McIntosh be charged with murder. The general turned himself in and during his trial argued that Gwinnett's death was due to poor medical care. He was acquitted but such was the fury directed against him in Savannah, he requested of General Washington that he be assigned in another area for the duration of the War for Independence. His brother died before he could be brought to trial. Lachlan McIntosh returned to Savannah after the war, but was not able to fully restore his plantation and business destroyed by the British. He lived in relative poverty and died in 1806.

Some have concluded that the disputes between Gwinnett and McIntosh and their supporters were a distraction in preparing Savannah's defenses against the British leading to the city's capture in 1778. Hugh McCall in his History of Georgia published in 1816, described Gwinnett's character thus, "Gwinnett appears to be a man of considerable literary talents, but hasty in his decisions, overbearing in his temper, and wild and excentric (sic) in his plans." George Walton, a fellow Georgia signer, considered him to be argumentative and egotistical. Another contemporary stated that his ambitions stretched beyond his abilities. There's a description one could use in many situations today.

Button Gwinnett's death may have been the end of his life, but it was just the beginning of perhaps one of Georgia's biggest mysteries. Where was Button buried? No one knows for certain. In fact, he is the only one of the fifty-six signers of the Declaration whose grave in uncertain, at least for some. When he died, his body was buried in the Christ Church burial ground, today known as the Colonial Cemetery. During the Civil War, however, many of the headstones in the cemetery, including Gwinnett's, were destroyed by Union troops. In the late 1950's, a search to find the grave was begun, some bones were found and, based on a damaged femur bone, considered to be those of Button Gwinnett. When a local doctor who had considerable experience in archeology examined them, he declared them to be those of a female. The bones were sent to the Smithsonian Museum and their experts also said that they were the bones of a female and that the break in the femur occurred after burial.

In 1960, the Mayor of Augusta requested the bones be sent there for burial under the Signers' Monument to join those of Lyman hall and George Walton. Savannahians were not going to give up Gwinnett (or the anonymous female) and refused. Meanwhile, the bones rested for over five years in the guest room of Capt. Arthur Funk, one of those convinced of their authenticity. One has to wonder how often the Captain hosted other guests. Finally, the mayor and city council made the decision that the remains were indeed those of Gwinnett and during a ceremony on October, 19, 1964, they were interred under a large Greek revival monument in the Colonial cemetery.

Is Button really there?

Button Gwinnett died owing a considerable amount of money. Today, however, his signature is the most sought after and ironically the most expensive to acquire of any in the United States. Because he signed so few documents, died at a relatively young age and because collectors are desirous of acquiring the signatures of all fifty-six signers of the Declaration, astronomical amounts are offered for this signature.

Button Gwinnett

In 2012, one was sold for almost $800,000.

Gwinnett County was named for the signer in 1918 and the eleventh Liberty ship launched at the Southeastern Shipbuilding Corporation during World War II was given the name, "S. S. Button Gwinnett".

The mid-line of Gwinnett Street also forms the northern boundary of the National Victorian District so designated in 1974. The area was developed after the Civil War to alleviate the crowded conditions in the Historic District and was facilitated by technological advances such as street paving, a street car system and electricity. The architecture differs from that in the Historic District in that most of the houses are of frame construction which because of two very destructive fires was no longer permitted in new builds in the Historic District. Frame construction was also cheaper making it possible for more families to live in the city. The District's borders are Gwinnett Street to Anderson in the south and Martin Luther King Jr. Boulevard on the west and East Broad on the east.

FURTHERMORE

There were other streets laid out during the colonial period named for people who were important to Georgia, but located outside of the boundaries of the National Historic District; Zubly and Fahm on the West Side, McIntosh and Wheaton on the East. Throughout the city there are streets named for famous Georgians, Southerners and other Americans. Washington. Eisenhower, Derenne, LaRoche and the many Confederate generals are just a few. Since people have congregated in villages, towns and cities they have given names to their streets honoring people, places, battles, boundaries, commerce or industry, topographical features and family members. The founding fathers of the Colony of Georgia and the new State of Georgia did the same. Today, one may question their selection of which leaders should have streets named for them and which should not, but those were their times, their circumstances and their choices. Perhaps because of their choices, it is possible to know and better understand Savannah's rich history.

APPENDIX A

SEVERAL DISTINGUISHED NOTABLES FOR WHOM NO STREETS WERE NAMED

TOMOCHICHI

Tomochichi and of the members of his Yamacraw tribe meeting the Trustees of the Colony of Georgia in London in 1734
Painting by Willem Verelst

Tomochichi, was the elderly mico (chief) of the Yamacraws, a small unit of the Creek Nation whose tribe occupied the lands on which the settlers had chosen for the new colony. Tomochichi facilitated the arrival of these first Georgia colonists and through his warm relationship with James Oglethorpe, food and land were provided for the English settlers. The mico would serve until his death in 1739 as an emissary for the English to the larger Creek Nation and without his assistance, the chances of the colony surviving would have been extremely low.

Before the chief died at the approximate age of 95 in 1739, he asked that he be buried in the town among his English friends and he was interred in the middle of Wright Square under a large pile of stones. The grave was shamefully destroyed in 1883 when a monument to the founder of the Central of Georgia Railroad, William Gordon, was erected on the site.

Charles C. Jones, Jr, in his *History of Savannah* published in 1890, wrote of his distress that no monument to the mico had been erected.

Nearly one hundred and fifty years have elapsed since these funeral honors were paid, and the monument ordered by General Oglethorpe has never been erected...Neither street nor public square perpetuates the name of this mico, and his memory dwells only in occasional recollection. This should not be. May we not hope for the sake of her reputation, in response to the wish of the founder of the colony of Georgia, and in glad acknowledgement of the debt of gratitude she owes to this noted Indian, that Savannah-herself a living witness of the enterprise, courage and taste of General Oglethorpe, a city which has rendered such conspicuous tribute to the memories of Greene, and Pulaski, and Jasper and the Confederate dead—will, at no distant day, cause to be lifted in one of her high places a suitable monument in just and honorable appreciation of the friendship and worthy deeds of the venerable Tomochichi?

In 1897, a motion to change the name of West Broad Street to Tomochichi Street was introduced in the Savannah city Council, but was defeated.

Two years later, Col. Jones's wish was fulfilled. The destruction of Tomochichi's grave so enraged William Gordon's daughter-in-law, Nellie Gordon, that she as president of the Colonial Dames of America had a large granite boulder placed in the square with a bronze plaque to honor the chief. The boulder was ordered from the Stone Mountain Co. in Atlanta who offered to provide it free of charge. Nellie wrote back saying that the Colonial Dames wanted the activity to be their contribution to Savannah and requested a bill. When it arrived, it was for one dollar, "payable on the Day of Judgment". Nellie sent the one dollar anyway saying that she "and the other ladies would be entirely too busy attending to their affairs on that momentous day".

Tomochichi's role in the founding of the colony is remembered with appreciation during the annual Georgia Day Pageant in Savannah. In 2005 the Federal Building and United States Courthouse erected on Wright Square between 1884 and 1889 and designed in the Second Renaissance Revival style, was renamed the Tomochichi Federal Building.

MARY MUSGROVE

Probably one of the more accurate depictions of Mary as she wore English clothing most of the time

Over the years, historians have compared Mary Musgrove to Pocahontas of Jamestown fame or Sacagawea who assisted Lewis and Clark in their explorations of the American West. She was, in fact, neither, but rather a very complex woman in her own right. She was also not the compliant, docile person generally depicted wearing buckskins, (the dress of the Plains Indians not the Creeks), in the annual Georgia Day pageants in Savannah and throughout the State. Born as Coosaponakeesa near where Macon is today, to a Creek mother and an English father, she spent her first seven years in the Creek Nation, but then the family moved to South Carolina where she was baptized and attended an English school. She took the name Mary after hearing the stories from Bible read to her by her father.

Mary's father was killed during the Yamassee War and she was orphaned. At about the age of seventeen she married John Musgrove, a half Creek trader and planter and together they purchased five hundred acres near her childhood home where they raised cattle and planted rice. The couple maintained their relationship with the Creek Indians and using their knowledge of both cultures were of great assistance to both.

In 1732 the Musgroves moved to a site on Yamacraw Bluff and when Oglethorpe and the first colonists landed there a year later were in a position to be interpreters and facilitators for the new arrivals. When John died in 1735, Mary, now very wealthy, became the chief interpreter, mediator and advisor performing an invaluable service to the new colony.

Mary's second husband was Jacob Matthews, an indentured servant to her first husband and a problem. She began having financial difficulties and with Jacob, started to press the local government for fees for her interpreting and titles from the English government to lands gifted her by the Creek Nation. The first claim, at least, was legitimate as Oglethorpe had promised her one hundred pounds per year for that task. Jacob died in 1742 with no resolution to either claim. Enter now her third husband, the Rev. Thomas Bosomworth, an educated cleric who some said practiced his profession only when it suited him. Also described as a gifted litigator, he expanded Mary's claims to include the islands of St. Catherine's, Sapelo and Ossabaw.

When in 1749 there had still been no resolution to any of these claims, the Bosomworths and about seventy-five Creek warriors arrived at Savannah to claim gifts from the British government, but also to provide a not-so-veiled threat to the colony. Fearing an Indian uprising, the colony's militia was called out and the confrontation ended peaceably. Mary, however, became even angrier and after many public outbursts was arrested several times and again the militia patrolled the streets fearing an attack. Mary was fired as interpreter and she and her husband moved to South Carolina to take up similar positions there.

After several more years of pressing their demands, a resolution was finally obtained with the Georgia governor, Henry Ellis. Mary was paid £2100 for her years of interpreting and given the title to St Catherine's Island. She and her husband lived on the island until her death in 1765.

Eighteenth and nineteenth century historians have characterized Mary as a heroine, a villain or both. Some have said that she was a simple woman led astray by her second and third husbands for their own financial gain. In reality she was instead a shrewd and astute businesswoman who between marriages ran several successful trading posts on her own. Matthews and Bosomworth probably assisted Mary with her fight for land and compensation rather than instigating these struggles. Mary was intelligent, and she was in the right place at the right time. Life in the colony would certainly have been much more difficult without her skills in interpreting, diplomacy and knowledge of the Creek Nation and one has to wonder if the Colony of Georgia would have survived at all without her contributions and assistance.

While no street in the Historic District was named after Mary Musgrove, there is a Mary Musgrove Drive on Wilmington Island and in November 2012, the new ferry, "Mary Musgrove", began operating from River Street across the Savannah River to Hutchinson Island.

DR. SAMUEL NUNEZ (NUNES)

Born Diogo Nunez Robeiro in Portugal in the late 1660's, Nunez was a well-respected physician who for a time served the Portuguese Grand Inquisitor. As crypto Jew, one who complied with orders to convert to Christianity, but practiced Judaism in private, Nunez and his family eventually had to escape to Britain to avoid the Inquisition. There he assumed the name Samuel, and worked for a brief period as a physician to the poor of the Bevis Marks congregation. Prominent British Jews were concerned that the number of Jewish immigrants coming into the country would overtake their ability to care for them and about possible repercussions from the Christian community so funds were raised to transport forty-two including the Nunez family, to the new colony of Georgia.

This group landed in the colony in July of 1733, just five

months after the first colonists and they weren't expected. The Trustees of the colony were explicit in denying the entrance of Catholics and had implied that no Jews should be accepted either. Oglethorpe was in a quandary. There was nothing actually written in the charter regarding Jews, but the colonists had been struck by an epidemic and the doctor who had arrived with the original settlers had died along with twenty-eight of the other original 114 colonists. The fact that there was a doctor in this group helped to sway the Colonel's decision to allow them to stay.

Dr. Nunez who was a specialist in infectious diseases, treated the ill and many survived. Oglethorpe then requested that the doctor be employed as the colony's physician to which the Trustees agreed even granting a salary, but told the colony's founder that the Jews were not to be allowed permanent residency. Oglethorpe ignored this and several months later allowed Dr. Nunez and several other families to acquire land. The Trustees later realized the value of having colonists such as Dr. Nunez and sent him medical supplies which allowed him to not only care for the sick, but to also open the first pharmacy in Georgia.

The doctor and his family successfully settled in, and in spite of language differences between the Sephardic and Ashkenazic Jews helped to establish the Temple Mickve Israel which has survived as the oldest Jewish synagogue in the South. Nunez was befriended by John Wesley who asked him to teach him Spanish (all the while attempting to convert the doctor to Christianity).

The current Temple Mickve Israel constructed in 1878

When Britain and Spain became involved in 1739 in The War of Jenkins' Ear, the Sephardic Jews in the colony became fearful of being burned at the stake for apostasy if the Spanish captured the Colony of Georgia. Many fled to the interior and some including Dr. Nunez and his family moved to Charleston. They then moved on to New York where he died in 1744 at the age of 76. Many of his descendants became famous in a variety of fields. The threat of the Inquisition brought Dr. Nunez to Georgia and ironically also later forced him to leave.

Even though his care of the colonists probably saved the colony, no street in the Historic District was named for Dr. Nunez. There is, however, a Nunez Street in the area south of Victory Drive and west of Skidaway Road. There is also a small community in Emanuel County named after the doctor.

GEORGE WALTON

George Walton

Geo Walton.

One would think that the next west to east street following Hall and Gwinnett would be Walton Street thus grouping the three signers of the Declaration of Independence together. It wasn't, and in fact no street in the Historic District was named for George Walton.

Walton was indeed one of the three Georgia signers. Some historians have said that he was the youngest delegate to the Second Continental Congress to sign the document, but because there is no consensus as to his birth date, somewhere between 1740 and 1749, this is difficult to ascertain. What is certain is that he was born in Virginia and moved to Georgia in 1768 to study law. He was admitted to the Bar in 1774 and became a very successful lawyer.

Very early on he joined the independence movement and was elected to the Provisional Council, then chosen to be president of the Committee of Public Safety in 1775. He, along with Button Gwinnett and Lyman Hall were selected as Georgia's representatives to the Continental Congress where they signed the document which declared, "...That these united colonies are and of Right ought to be Free and Independent States...".

Returning to Savannah, Walton was commissioned a colonel in the First Regiment of the Georgia militia. He was wounded in the defense of the city in 1778 and captured by the British. He was later exchanged for a British naval officer even though the fifty-six signers of the Declaration had been declared traitors and were to be hanged if caught.

Returning to the State of Georgia after the war, Walton served two short terms as governor, six years as Chief Justice then as a Superior Court Judge, and was then chosen to complete the United States Senate term of James Jackson. He was, however, not re-elected and retired to his home near Augusta to farm.

Throughout his career Walton was involved in various political disputes, the most famous being that between General Lachlan McIntosh and Button Gwinnett which led to the duel in which McIntosh killed Gwinnett. Walton had sided with McIntosh and was censured by the State Legislature for his role in the duel. He later turned on his former friend whose son publicly horse whipped him.

George Walton died on February 2, 1804 and was buried in the Rosney Cemetery. In 1848, his body was re-interred at the Signers Monument in Augusta. The intention was to have all three of the signers buried there and Lyman Hall's body was re-interred under the monument, but with the controversy at the time regarding the actual location of Button Gwinnett's remains, Walton was spared the possibility of spending eternity next to his enemy.

While no Savannah street or square in the Historic District was named for George Walton, Walton County near Atlanta, a prominent street in Augusta and high schools in Marietta and Monroe, Georgia were given his name as was the fourth Liberty ship launched at the Southeastern Shipbuilding Corporation in Savannah during World War II.

GEORGE WASHINGTON

George Washington
Portrait by Gilbert Stuart

No street in the Historic District was named for the Commander-in-Chief of the American forces in the Revolutionary War, the first President of the United States and the legendary "Father of his Country". Washington Square laid out in 1790 does recognize him, as does the much later constructed Washington Avenue located further south in the Ardsley Park residential area of the city. Of course his name has been given to a State, the Nation's Capital, parks, streets, universities, and thousands of children over the years. Monuments to his memory have been erected throughout the country and his face appears on Mt Rushmore, on the one dollar bill and of course on many postage stamps.

THE EARL OF EGMONT

John Perceval, 1st Earl of Egmont
By John Faber Jr. After Hans Hysing

While John Perceval, First Earl of Egmont never set foot in the Colony of Georgia, he was second in importance only to James Oglethorpe in the establishing of the Colony. Born in 1683 in County Cork, Ireland, Perceval was elected to the British House of Commons in 1727 and a year later became a member of the committee investigating prison conditions. Oglethorpe, too, was a member of that committee and the two became friends and the motivating force in creating the Trustees for the Establishment of the Colony of Georgia in America. When the charter for the colony was approved in 1732, Perceval was made president of the Trustees and he used his money, time and influence to insure the success of the Colony.

In 1733, the year of the founding of the Colony of Georgia, Perceval was made Earl of Egmont in the peerage of Ireland. He, on three occasion turned down offers of British peerage. Lord Egmont died in London in May 1748.

While no street was named for this strong supporter of the new Colony, one of the original squares did bear his name...at least for a while. The square was later renamed Wright Square in honor of Georgia's last colonial governor.

NOBLE JONES

Noble Jones

As mentioned earlier, many residents of Savannah probably assume that Jones Street was named for Noble Jones or perhaps his son, Noble Wimberly Jones. In fact no street was named for either which is strange as both were certainly worthy.

Noble Jones was a carpenter born in Herefordshire in 1702. He, with his wife and their son and daughter arrived on the ship, Anne, with Oglethorpe and the original colonists in February 1733. A man "of vast energy and talent", he would hold positions throughout the life of the colony as a surveyor, carpenter, builder, Indian Agent, constable, physician and military officer, and planter.

As a physician, he stepped in after Dr. Cox, the colony's only trained doctor died just months after arrival, to treat the victims of what was probably a typhoid epidemic. His only training came from watching and assisting Dr. Cox on the voyage to America. Unfortunately, his treatment using Indian Root, rhubarb and laudanum did not save many and the propitious arrival of Dr. Nunez probably saved the colony. Jones did train his son in the medical arts and Noble Wimberly Jones did become a very successful physician.

James Oglethorpe appointed Jones as an officer in the Georgia Militia and the two fought together against the Spanish in Florida during the War of Jenkin's Ear. It was Jones' marine scouts who provided the information which allowed General Oglethorpe to defeat the Spanish invasion of Georgia at the Battle of Bloody Marsh. In the colony's military review in 1751, it was Col. Jones who led the 220 militiamen in the parade.

His success in his various positions allowed him to advance to an elevated rank in the colony and provided him with the means to develop a large land grant some eight miles from Savannah into Wormsloe Plantation, today a State Park open to the public. Colonial Georgians, always looking for an interesting event, visited Wormsloe during a period of eight days in 1765 to view an agave plant (also known as the Century Plant) with beautiful blossoms on thirty-three branches.

During the build-up to the War of Independence, Noble Jones remained loyal to the Royal Governor, James Wright, although his son became a fierce advocate of independence. Jones died on November 2, 1775 on the eve of the Revolution.

NOBLE WIMBERLY JONES

Noble Wimberley Jones
Portrait by Charles Wilson Peale

Noble Wimberly Jones was a leading Georgia patriot in the

American Revolution. Born in Lambeth, England in 1723, he immigrated to the colony of Georgia with his family at the age of ten. The son of the famous Georgia colonial, Noble Jones, he was known to most by his full name to distinguish him from his father. As a youth, Noble Wimberly Jones served in the militia under General Oglethorpe and studied medicine with his father. In 1755 he married Sarah Davis and the couple had fourteen children only one of which survived them. That son, George would later become a U. S. Senator.

That same year, 1755, Jones began his political career, but unlike his father who was a confirmed Royalist, he was an ardent Whig, a supporter of independence. He was elected to the Commons House of Assembly and served until the beginning of the Revolution. In 1768, as Speaker of the House he secured the services of Benjamin Franklin to represent the colony in London. He and Franklin would remain life-long friends. Jones' activities were seen as a threat by the Royal Governor, James Wright, who dissolved the assembly and continued to do so every time Jones was elected Speaker. Following the passage by Parliament of the Intolerable Acts in 1775, Jones and others formed the short-lived Provincial Congress. He was elected to attend the Second Continental Congress, but did not attend because of insufficient public support and the illness of his father who died that year. When the news of the Battles of Lexington and Concord reached Georgia, a group of Whigs which included Jones broke into the local powder magazine and while keeping some gunpowder for use against the British in the colony, much was sent to Boston which, it is said, was used at the battle of Bunker Hill.

When the royal governor was forced to flee the colony, Jones assisted in the writing of the 1777 State Constitution and was elected Speaker of the new House of Assembly. He fled to Charleston when the British captured Savannah and was taken prisoner several years later when that city, too, was captured. Jones was held captive in St. Augustine, Florida until he was exchanged in 1781, and transferred to Philadelphia. There he served as a Georgia delegate to the Continental Congress.

Returning to Savannah in 1882, he was elected Speaker of the Georgia House and continued his medical practice, becoming the first president of the newly formed Georgia Medical Society. He was considered to be an outstanding physician and apparently thought nothing of riding forty miles on horseback to treat a patient.

Noble Wimberly Jones died on January 9, 1805 and was buried in Bonaventure Cemetery.

JOHN WESLEY

John Wesley by William Hamilton

John Wesley's sojourn in Savannah was not the highlight of his career. At the request of James Oglethorpe, he and his brother Charles sailed for the Colony of Georgia where Charles was appointed Secretary of Indian Affairs, and sent to be chaplain to the garrison on St. Simon's Island while John was to be the minister of the new parish in Savannah.

Charles had difficulty being accepted by the colonists and in July of 1736 was sent to London with dispatches to the Trustees. He never returned to Georgia. John considered himself to be a High Churchman and saw Georgia as an opportunity to establish "primitive Christianity in a primitive environment". His ministry was controversial and while he was able to increase church attendance and establish small groups of believers, his ministry was judged to be less than successful both by others and himself. He stated later that, "He who went to America to convert others was himself never converted to God".

To add to his problems, he fell in love with a young woman named Sophia Hopkey who ended up marrying someone else. He considered this to be a loss of faith on her part and denied her communion. As a result, legal proceedings were taken against him, and to avoid them he left Georgia and returned to England in December 1737. While in Georgia, one of his most significant accomplishments was the publication of a *Collection of Psalms and Hymns*, the first Anglican hymnal published in America.

If his two years in Savannah weren't his best, Wesley's career after that was certainly much more successful and he is credited as being the founding father of Methodism. He was born in 1703, one of fifteen children of an Anglican minister and his wife. He graduated from Oxford determined to become a minister. and was ordained on September 22, 1728. He decided early on that to reach as many people as possible it would be necessary to travel and preach out of doors. Speaking at times to crowds of up to 20,000 people it is said that during his life he traveled more than 250,000 miles and preached more than 40,000 times.

Wesley's preaching was not always welcomed by local

priests and while he considered that his interpretation of theology fitted well within the Anglican Church, church leaders disagreed and the breach between the two gradually widened. He was, however, widely respected and towards the end of his life was considered by some to be, "the best loved man in England".

John Wesley died on March 2, 1791 at the age of eighty-seven. Reportedly, his last words were, *The best of all is, God is with us."* He was entombed at Wesley's Chapel in London.

No street in Savannah was named for John Wesley, but the Wesley Monumental Church on Calhoun Square in Savannah was and a statue was dedicated to him in Reynolds Square in 1969, honoring him for his role in founding the Methodist Religion, but probably not for his activities in Savannah.

John Wesley Statue in Reynolds Square

GEORGE WHITEFIELD

George Whitefield

George Whitefield's interest in establishing an orphanage in Savannah was probably influenced by his childhood. He was born in 1714, in a tavern in a rough area of Gloucester and was impoverished as a child. His father, the tavern keeper, died when he was just two, but his mother made sure that he received a good education. He entered Oxford as a servitor, the lowest rank of students and was assigned as a servant to the wealthy students.

At Oxford, Whitefield met John and Charles Wesley, joined their Holy Club (Methodist group) and made the decision to become a priest. At the age of twenty-two, he graduated and was ordained at Gloucester Cathedral. When he began to preach he found that large groups were attracted to both his message and his manner. Though small in stature and a bit cross-eyed, he was charismatic, had a beautiful voice that carried great distances and he was very dramatic. All of this was probably developed through a career on the stage during his youth.

Whitefield became more and more popular and used the media of the day to build that popularity. Crowds of twenty to thirty thousand turned up to hear him preach. Benjamin Franklin wrote after hearing one of Whitefield's sermons,

...I perceived that he intended to finish with a collection and I silently resolved that he get nothing from me. I had in my pocket a handful of copper money, three or four silver dollars and five pistols (coins) of gold. As he proceeded I began to soften and I concluded to give the coppers. Another stroke of his oratory made me ashamed of that and determined me to give the silver; and he finished so admirably that I emptied my pockets into the collector's dish, gold and all.

The Wesleys invited Whitefield to join them in the new Georgia colony which he did, arriving in May 1738. During his brief stay, he made the decision to build an orphanage and then returned to England to preach and to raise funds for this project. In late 1739, Whitefield arrived in Philadelphia and began travelling throughout the colonies, preaching to huge crowds and collecting money. He arrived in Savannah to a hero's welcome and with over £2500 to begin construction of the orphanage he would call Bethesda (which means "House of Mercy"). After laying the first brick, Whitefield left much of the supervision of construction and the eventual running of Bethesda to James Habersham, who had come to Georgia to become a missionary at Whitefield's request.

George Whitefield would make seven trips to America and travelled throughout Scotland, Ireland and even making trips to Bermuda, Gibraltar and the Netherlands, always drawing great numbers of the faithful. He preached his last sermon on the day before he died. Death came on September 30, 1770 in Newburyport, Massachusetts and he was buried in a crypt under the pulpit of the Old South Presbyterian Church. In his will, he left Bethesda to Selina Countess of Huntingdon who had been a major sponsor of the orphanage. No street in Savannah was named for George Whitefield, but the last of the squares developed in the Historic district bears his name.

APPENDIX B

NAMES OF THE SQUARES

Savannah's twenty two squares are the result of the innovative and far-reaching plan drawn up by the founder of the Colony of Georgia, James Edward Oglethorpe. Originally designed to provide open spaces for the early residents to congregate, tether livestock and an opportunity for the militias to train, they have become "The Jewels" of the city.

The first four squares were laid out in 1733 by Oglethorpe with assistance from Col. Bull.

1. **Johnson Square.** Named for Robert Johnson, Governor of South Carolina who provided so much early assistance to the Georgia colonists.

2. **Wright Square.** Originally named Perceval Square in honor of John Perceval, a member of the Trustees and friend of Oglethorpe who was an early supporter of the General's plans for the colony. It was known among some in the colony as the Hanging Square and was the location for the hanging of Alice Riley, the first woman in the colony to be executed for murder.

It was renamed in 1763 to honor the colony's third and last Royal governor, Sir James Wright. It has also been known as Post Office Square and Court House Square.

3. **Ellis Square.** Named for Henry Ellis, the second Royal governor. It has also been known as Market Square.

4. **Telfair Square.** Originally named St. James Square after the park in London, this square was renamed in 1883 to honor the Telfair family which included Edward Telfair a State governor, Thomas Telfair, a U. S. Congressman and Mary Telfair, benefactor of the Telfair Academy of Arts and Sciences, The Georgia Historical Society and the Telfair Hospital. This square is the only one named for a family rather than an individual.

The next two squares were established while Oglethorpe was still in the colony.

5. **Reynolds Square.** Created in 1734 and originally named Lower New Square, it was renamed for John Reynolds, the governor of the colony in the mid 1750's. Arguably the least popular of the colonial governors, it is strange that a square was named for him. Reynolds hated Savannah saying that Oglethorpe had selected the wrong site, a comment which did not endear him to locals. As a result, as Chan Sieg recorded in his fine book, "The Squares: An Introduction to Savannah", "the party for his arrival was only exceeded by that over his departure".

6. **Oglethorpe Square.** This square was originally named Upper New Square, but was later renamed for the founder of the colony.

As the town grew east and west along the river and to the south, Oglethorpe's plan of creating wards and squares was continued.

7. **Washington Square.** Laid out in 1790 and named for the new country's first president, this site was the scene of one of Savannah's largest events, the first Fourth of July Celebration. During the first half of the Nineteenth century it was also the location for the city's largest annual New Year's Eve celebrations.

8. **Franklin Square.** Laid out in 1790, but not named until the following year, this square was one of three opened to traffic on Montgomery Street in the 1930's, ostensibly to ease traffic congestion. Named for Benjamin Franklin who besides being the American Colonies' representative in France during the Revolutionary War, a signer of the Declaration of Independence and an inventor of note, was Georgia's personal agent in Britain from 1768 to 1775. The square exists today only as two slivers of grass on either side of Montgomery Street.

9. **Warren Square.** The naming of this square in 1791 for General Joseph Warren of Massachusetts who was killed at the Battle of Bunker Hill was an indication of the close relationship between Savannah and Boston at that time. Much of the powder used by the Continental troops at that battle had been captured by the Liberty Boys in Savannah and shipped north where the fighting was heaviest in the early stages of the war.

10. **Columbia Square.** One of three squares established in 1799, this square was named for Columbia, the poetic female personification of the United States. Some have speculated that the

selection of this name was to celebrate the creation by an act of Congress in 1790 of the District of Columbia as the nation's capital.

11. **Greene Square.** Also laid out in 1799 this square was named for General Nathaniel Greene, commander of the southern Continental forces during the Revolutionary War. In 1785, Greene settled on his plantation, Mulberry Grove, fourteen miles north of Savannah. Given to him by a grateful nation, Mulberry Grove became famous eight years later as the site where Eli Whitney invented the cotton gin.

12. **Liberty Square.** The third square established in 1799, it was also one of the three paved over for improvements to Montgomery Street. Named for the Savannah Liberty Boys of Revolutionary War fame and to celebrate the victory over the British, all that remains of this square is a small grassy area in front of the court house and jail and another directly across Montgomery Street.

13. **Elbert Square.** Created in 1781 and named for Samuel Elbert, a Revolutionary soldier, Sheriff of Chatham County and Governor of Georgia, this square, too, was also paved over as an improvement to Montgomery Street and exists today as only a narrow strip across Montgomery Street from the Civic Center.

14. **Chippewa Square.** One of two squares referencing the War of 1812, this square created in 1815, honors the American soldiers killed at the Battle of Chippewa during the invasion of Canada. Among other important buildings, this square hosts the Savannah Theater, the oldest theater in continuous use in America although a more modern building has replaced the

original designed by William Jay.

15. **Orleans Square.** This square commemorates the victory of General Andrew Jackson over the British at the Battle of New Orleans. Established in 1815, it fronts the Savannah Civic Center and on the opposite side, the McAlpin-Fowlkes House.

16. **Lafayette Square.** One of three squares created in 1837, this square honors the French hero of the Revolutionary War, the Marquis de Lafayette. In March of 1825, Lafayette visited Savannah where he laid the cornerstone for the monument to General Nathaniel Greene in Johnson Square. In 1888, the first electric street lights were tested and placed into operation in this square.

17. **Pulaski Square.** Named for General Casimir Pulaski the Polish-born cavalry leader killed at the Siege of Savannah in 1779, Pulaski Square was laid out in 1837. For some reason his statue was placed in Monterey Square even though there is no monument in Pulaski Square.

18. **Madison Square.** This is the square that can boast that Sherman slept here. Actually, the general slept in the Green-Meldrim House which stands on the northwest trust lot of the square. Laid out in 1837 and named for James Madison, the fourth president of the United States, the monument in this square commemorates Sargent Jasper who died heroically during the Siege of Savannah in the Revolutionary War. The two cannons at the south boundary represent the starting point of the first two highways in Georgia, the Louisville Road to Darien and the Augusta Road to Augusta.

19. **Crawford Square.** Named for William Harris Crawford who was the secretary of the Treasury under James Madison and considered the front runner in the presidential election of 1824 until concerns over his health resulted in John Quincy Adams being elected. Created in 1841, it was during the years of segregation the only square where African Americans were allowed to congregate. Today, it is the only square with playground facilities.

20. **Chatham Square.** Established in 1847 and named for William Pitt, the First Earl of Chatham, an early supporter of the Georgia Colony, and an opponent of Parliament during the Revolutionary War. This square was once the playground for the Barnard Street Elementary School which was bought by the Savannah College of Art and Design and is, today, used as one of its classroom buildings. Considered by some today as a "neighborhood square" its lovely moss-draped trees provide a tranquil, quiet setting for both residents and tourists.

21. **Monterey Square.** When the Irish Jasper Greens returned in 1847 from the war with Mexico, Savannahians who have always been proud of their military units, named the square to commemorate the capture of the City of Monterrey (correct spelling) by American forces under General Zachary Taylor. As mentioned earlier, the monument to Count Casimir Pulaski is the centerpiece of this square.

22. **Troop Square.** Created in 1851 and named for George Michael Troop, a governor of Georgia and member of the House of the U. S. Representatives and the Senate, this square is one of two named for living persons, the other being Washington

Square. One of its special features is a water fountain for dogs.

23. **Calhoun Square.** Named for South Carolinian, John C. Calhoun who served as Secretary of War, Secretary of State and Vice President under both John Quincy Adams and Andrew Jackson, this square was laid out in 1851. For many years the east side of the square served as a playground for Massie Elementary School, the oldest public school in the State. This is the only square around which all of the original buildings are still intact.

24. **Whitefield Square.** Created in 1851, this was the last square laid out and with Chatham, Monterey, Calhoun Squares forms the southern and final boundary of the continuation of General Oglethorpe's plan for the city. It was named for George White-field who was known as "The Great Evangelist" in colonial times and was the founder of the Bethesda Home for Boys, the first orphanage in America. The centerpiece, a lovely gazebo, has been the site for many weddings.

Forsyth Park. As the city continued to expand to the south, no additional squares were laid out, but the creation of Forsyth Park was intended to serve the new southern portion of the city. Originally, this land bordered by Gaston Street on the north, Whitaker on the west and Drayton on the east, had in 1840 been set aside and enclosed as a park "for the pleasure of the public" by William Hodgson and was referred to as Hodgson Park. In 1851, Georgia Governor, John Forsyth donated twenty acres to extend the park further south and the park was renamed for him. The northern end is landscaped, featuring wide walkways and benches under a canopy of oaks, magnolias and many other species of trees.

The centerpiece of the park is its fountain erected in 1858. It was a model selected from an ironworks catalogue which was based on a fountain at the Place de la Concorde in Paris.

The southern portion of the park, originally used as drill fields for militias, today features basketball and tennis courts, and areas for rugby, soccer and frisbee.

It is interesting that the monuments for several historic figures were not placed in the squares that bear their names. The statue of James Oglethorpe was not placed in Oglethorpe Square, but in Chippewa Square. That of General Nathaniel Green is in Johnson Square rather than Green Square and the obelisk commemorating the life of Casimir Pulaski is not in Pulaski Square, but in Monterey Square.

A full description of the squares accompanied by magnificent black and white photographs can be found in Chan Sieg's lovely book, "The Squares: An Introduction to Savannah". There are also many books, brochures and pamphlets available from Savannah's many tourist organizations.

INDEX OF STREET NAMES

SELECTED SOURCES

BOOKS

Bell, Jr. Malcolm and Jane Isley. *Historic Savannah.* Morris Newspaper Corporation. Savannah. 1977.

Coleman, Kenneth. *Colonial Georgia: A History.* Charles Scribner and Sons. New York. 1926.

Daiss, Timothy. *Rebels Saints and Sinners: Savannah's Rich history and Colorful Personalities.* Pelican publishing Co. Gretna, Louisiana. 2002.

Davis, Harold E. *The Fledgling Province: Social and Cultural Life in Colonial Georgia 1733-1776.* University of North Carolina Press. Chapel Hill. 1976.

Estill, J.L. *A Guide to Strangers Visiting Savannah for Business, Health or Pleasure.* Morning News Steam Printing House. Savannah. 1851.

Ettinger, Amos Aschbach. *James Edward Oglethorpe: Imperial Idealist.* Clarendon Press. Oxford. 1936.

Fertig, Barbara C. *City of Savannah Manual for the Instruction and Licensing of Tour Guides in the City of Savannah.* City of Savannah. 2006.

Fraser, Jr., Walter G. *Savannah in the Old South.* University of Georgia Press. Athens. 2005.

Gamble Jr., Thomas. *A History of the City Government of Savannah*

Georgia from 1790 to 1901. Savannah, Georgia. 1900.

Garrison, Webb. *Oglethorpe's Folly: The Birth of Georgia.* Copple House Books. Lakemont, Georgia. 1977.

Giro, Christina M. *The Thirteen Colonies-Georgia.* Lucent Books, Inc. San Diego. 2002.

Gregory, G, A. *Savannah and its Surroundings.* Press of the Morning News. Savannah. 1890.

Henry, Charles S. *A Digest of all of the Ordinances of the City of Savannah which were in force on the first of July, 1851.* Savannah. 1854.

Hewatt, Alexander. *A Historical Account of the Rise and Progress of the Colonies of South Carolina and Georgia.* Volumes 1 and 2. Reprint by Aeterna. San Bernardino. 2010.

Heyward, Maude and Elizabeth V. McLaws. *Illustrated Guide to Savannah.* Savannah. 1910.

Hirsch, Arthur Henry. *The Huguenots of Colonial South Carolina.* Duke University Press. Durham. 1928.

Hough, Franklin Benjamin. *The Siege of Savannah by the Command of the Combined American and French Forces.* J. Munsell. Albany, N.Y. 1866.

Jackson, Harvey M. and Phinizy Spalding. ed. *Forty Years of Diversity: Essays on Colonial Georgia.* University of Georgia Press. Athens. 1984.

Jones, Charles Colcock, Jr. *History of Savannah, Georgia: From its Settlement to the Close of the Eighteenth Century.* D. Mason & Co. Syracuse, N.Y. 1890.

Lambert, Frank. *James Habersham: Loyalty, Politics and Commerce in Colonial Georgia.* University of Georgia Press. Athens. 2005.

Lane. Mills B. ed. *General Oglethorpe's Georgia: Colonial Letters 1733-1743.* Volumes 1 & 2. Beehive Press. Savannah. 1975.

Lee, F. D. and J. L. Agnew. *Historical Record of the City of Savannah.* Savannah Morning News Steam Powered Press. Savannah. 1869.

McCall, Captain Hugh. *History of Georgia.* Seymour Williams. Savannah. 1816.

Morrill, Dan L. *Southern Campaigns of the American Revolution.* The Nautical and Aviation Publishing Company of America. Mount Pleasant. South Carolina. 1993.

Morrison, Samuel Eliot. *Oxford History of the American People.* Oxford University Press. Oxford. 1965.

Russell, Preston and Barbara Hines. *Savannah: A History of her People since 1733.* Frederic C. Beil. Savannah. 1992.

___ *Savannah: a City of Opportunities.* The Savannah Morning News. Savannah. 1904.

___ *Savannah, Georgia: It's Advantages, Resources and Business Facilities.* The Morning News Print. Savannah. 1895.

Sharpe, Colin Gwinnett. *Button Gwinnett: Failed Merchant, Plantation Owner, Mountebank, Politician and Founding Father.* Youcaxton Publications. Oxford. 2013.

Sieg, Chan. *The Squares: An Introduction to Savannah.* The Donning Co. Norfolk. 1984.

Spaulding, Phinizy. *Oglethorpe in America.* University of Georgia Press. Athens. 1984.

Toledano, Roulhac. *The National Trust Guide to Savannah: Architectural and Cultural Treasures.* John Wiley and Sons, Inc. New York. 1997.

Weir, Robert M. *Colonial South Carolina: A History.* Kto Press. New York. 1983.

Wilson, Adelaide and Georgia Weymouth. *Historic and Picturesque Savannah.* Photogravure Company. Boston. 1889.

___ *Why Savannah?* Savannah Chamber of Commerce. Savannah. 1908.

UNPUBLISHED MANUSCRIPTS

Fling, H. Franklin. *William Gaston; The Stranger's Friend.* Paper for History 300. Armstrong Atlantic State University. 1989.

Lavelle, Brittany. *The Making of a Legacy: Three Generations of Drayton Family Women and their Influence on the Landscape of the Low Country and Ninetieth century Charleston.* Master's Thesis, Clemson University. Clemson, S. C. 2012.

Nyberg, Michele. Thomas U. P. Charlton. Paper for History 300. Armstrong Atlantic State University. 1989.

RESEARCH CENTERS

Archives of the City of Savannah. Savannah.

The Georgia Historical Society. Savannah.

The Hargrett Rare Book and Manuscript Library. The University of Georgia. Athens.

The Live Oak Library. Savannah

Tony Cope is a native of Savannah, Georgia, who retired after thirty years in public education, serving as a teacher, head baseball coach, administrator and creator and long-time director of the award winning environmental education facility, the Oatland Island Wildlife Center. He was a member of a long list of State and local boards, served three terms as president of the Savannah Symphony and was featured in the book *Movers and Shakers of Georgia*. He is the author of *On the Swing Shift: Building Liberty Ships in Savannah* published by the Naval Institute Press in 2009, *The House on Gaston: A Savannah Childhood* published in 2013, and *Stealing Stones* published in 2015, both by The Abercorn Press. In Ireland he has written the scripts for and performed in three highly acclaimed musical productions, *Moon River; A Reflection*, a tribute to Savannah's Johnny Mercer, *The Rat Pack and Friends* and *Tin Pan Alley: From Ragtime to Show Time*. He is also the co-author of *A History of the Mashie-Niblicks Golfing Society* published in 2012.

Tony lives with his wife, Ellen, and five cats near Kinsale in County Cork, Ireland, dividing his time between writing, playing golf (badly) and building dry stone walls.